THE THIRTEEN APOSTLES

J. ELLSWORTH KALAS

ABINGDON PRESS

NASHVILLE

THE THIRTEEN APOSTLES

Copyright © 2002 by Abingdon Press

This book is printed on acid-free paper.

Library of Congress Cataloging-in-Publication Data

Kalas, J. Ellsworth, 1923–
    The thirteen Apostles / J. Ellsworth Kalas.
        p.   cm.
    ISBN 0-687-09721-5 (alk. paper)
    1. Apostles.   I. Title

BS2440 .K35 2002
225.9'22—dc21   2001053563

Scripture quotations, unless otherwise noted, are from the New Revised Standard Version of the Bible. Copyright © 1989, by the Division of Christian Education of the National Council of the Churches of Christ in the United States of America. Used by permission.

Scripture quotations noted as KJV are from the King James or Authorized Version of the Bible.

Scripture quotations by J. B. Phillips are from *The New Testament in Modern English, Rev. Ed.* © J. B. PHILLIPS 1958, 1960, 1972 (New York: The Macmillan Company).

11 12 13 – 18 17 16 15 14 13 12

MANUFACTURED IN THE UNITED STATES OF AMERICA

To

Chris Zaffiras / Bill Travis,

for friendship that began

in Irving School, 1932,

and that through many times and places

continues still

Contents

$\mathcal{I}$ntroduction

Looking for a really difficult trivia question? See if anyone in your social gathering can name the twelve apostles. If anyone can, they'll probably *sing* the list because in some childhood day they mastered these twelve names with the help of a simple tune. But even those who can name the twelve are likely to be stumped when you ask the name of the thirteenth apostle.

Yet if ever in human history there has been one small group of persons who have left an utterly indelible impact on the world, it is this group. When Jesus departed our planet, he left his mission and message in the care of these persons: today, their spiritual descendants constitute the largest single religious body in the world.

They were a quite unlikely group. Saint Paul said that the treasure of the gospel has been entrusted to "clay jars, so that it may be made clear that this extraordinary power belongs to God and does not come from us" (2 Corinthians 4:7). If there were any doubt about Paul's statement, these thirteen men make it irrefutable. Yet today their names can be found in every part of the world—on churches, hospitals, homes for the aging, rescue missions, orphanages; and, of course, on tens of millions of persons. Every boy named John or Andrew, and every girl named Joan, Jean, or Andrea, gives testimony, wittingly or not, to the influence of this extraordinary group.

So I have written a book to help you know them better. I have tried to find the particular characteristic in each person that would seem to define that person most clearly. As you read their stories, you'll notice that I draw often upon the traditions and legends that have grown up around each one. I make no apology for this; I agree with the late Phyllis McGinley, who said in her book *Saint-Watching,* "Behind every myth lies a truth, behind every legend is reality." Most of the myths and legends draw upon some ancient story that no doubt had some historical origins. In every event I've tried to be clear about what is historical and what is not.

I owe several words of thanks. Janet Brown did a good deal of basic research to provide me with some background information on Matthias; I'm grateful to her for saved hours and for perceptive work. And I am indebted to Ruth Wolgemuth for a healthy push. She said, in a convincing tone, "The next time you write a book, write it on the twelve apostles." This was a subject on which I had already established a file, but that can be said for at least a dozen other subjects. Ruth's few words were persuasive, however, because I realized that she knows what the average church member is reading. So I went right to work on the idea. And, of course, I went her one better; I've written about the *thirteen* apostles.

I do not mean to sound superpious, but I pray over the books I write. I pray when I write them, pray as they are being edited, and pray as they are being bought and read. As you read this book, I pray that something about the lives of these thirteen storied figures will help both you and me to move a step closer to our Lord—the Lord who called them, and who has called you and me.

CHAPTER 1
ANDREW, A BROTHER

READ JOHN 1:35-42.

I would like to have had Andrew for a brother. If I had known the apostles, I would have chosen John for stimulating conversation, and Matthew for financial counsel. And Peter, of course, for outrageous talk, those remarks that push the boundaries of conversation. But for a friend and brother, I would choose Andrew.

Is that reason enough to use Andrew as the starting point for a book on the apostles? Not just of itself, perhaps, although when I look back on the patterns of my life, people who classify as friends and brothers and sisters rank very high in my catalog of value.

But of course the best reason for starting with Andrew is because Jesus did. According to the New Testament records, Andrew was the first of the Twelve whom Jesus called. Early church writings frequently refer to Andrew by the Greek title *Protokletos*, which means "first-called."

You and I might want to argue that Andrew was the first called. As far as I can see, he had little obvious claim to greatness. The Gospels of Matthew, Mark, and Luke mention him only to list his name among the Twelve. This is also the way he is mentioned in the book of Acts, and there just once. It is only John's Gospel that brings Andrew out of the background, even momentarily.

In the language of a dramatist, Andrew appears in the first

three Gospels and in Acts as someone listed in the crowd scenes. In the Gospel of John, he emerges three times as a supporting actor. But never, never does Andrew play a leading role. He is part of a larger group, or he is a supporting player, and that's it.

But a significant, beautiful word is almost always connected with the name of Andrew, and that word shows how great a soul he was: *Brother*. Andrew, a brother. As I've already said, Andrew is mentioned only a few times in the New Testament, and in a good share of these citings he is designated in this fashion: "Andrew, Simon Peter's brother." It's as if the writers were saying, "If you want to identify Andrew, here's the point of reference: He's a brother of the great Simon Peter."

With that statement I have probably demonstrated more clearly than ever that Andrew isn't the proper starting point for an apostolic study. If his only achievement is that he was a brother to a great man—well, unless you are a student of sibling rivalries you will figure that history is full of its Andrews. And most of them, of course, are unknown to us.

As you know, we use the word *brother* primarily in two ways. Sometimes it indicates a family relationship, to describe two persons who have the same parents or who are joined by adoption. If Andrew's only claim to the "brother" title were his blood tie with Simon Peter, the whole thing would be worth no more than a passing reference. But we also use the term in an emotional or a poetic sense, to describe someone with certain qualities of loyalty, compassion, and concern. Thus we say of some persons, "I tell you, when I was in trouble he was a real *brother* to me." Or we make an adjective of the quality and praise someone by saying, "He's a very brotherly sort."

I say all of this cautiously, since I'm a man, and these remarks may be seen as sexist prejudice. I'm not sure why "sisterly" has never gotten the same standing as "brotherly"; in truth, it may be because of a male-dominated culture. Or per-

haps it's because we men (at least we're told) don't form inti-
mate bonds as easily as women, so "brotherly" is a stronger
term because it is a more unlikely one. Yet I think of a woman
who said of a faithful friend, "I suppose it's an oxymoron, but
the only way I can rightly describe her is to say that she's been
brotherly when I've needed her."

In any event, this is what I'd like to say of Andrew. He was,
of course, Simon Peter's brother. But far more important, he
possessed the spirit of a brother. His spiritual bloodline was
exceedingly large.

Let me give you something of Andrew's background. He
was a native of Bethsaida, a village on the shore of the Sea of
Galilee. He was a son of Jonas and the brother of Simon, who
came to be called Peter. Since Andrew lived in a fishing town
on the shore of his country's main body of water, it was natural for him to take up the life of a fisherman. Apparently he
was in partnership with his father and brother. Perhaps the
sign read "Jonas and Sons, fishermen." Or perhaps the three
had been associated long enough that the sign read: "Jonas
and Simon and Andrew, sons of Jonas, fishermen."

Theirs was a rugged life, but rewarding in its own way. They
would fish all night, struggling with a boat that was often playfully tossed about by wind and waves, and wrestling with great
nets that had to repeatedly be thrown down into the water.
After a night of fishing, the men would take their fish to the
marketplace; perhaps more often than not they would return
to the seaside to repair their nets. Andrew probably knew little of the outside world. It's likely that he had never traveled
a dozen miles from Bethsaida and the Sea of Galilee, except
for feast day trips to Jerusalem.

But Andrew was a person of spiritual hunger. His soul was
on the search. When he heard about a peculiar preacher out
in the wilderness, John the Baptist, Andrew went to hear his
message of repentance and to see him baptize converts. He

became something of a disciple of the wilderness prophet. It's likely that he saw John as God's key person, but the Baptist himself continually advised the crowds that a greater one was coming, one who would baptize them with the Holy Spirit and with fire.

And one day Jesus of Nazareth came. John the Baptist pointed him out, calling him the Lamb of God who would take away the sin of the world. Immediately Andrew and another fisherman, John, followed Jesus. When Jesus sensed that they were trailing him, he turned and asked, "What do you seek?" Andrew and John—perhaps feeling a little like small boys who have been caught off-bounds—replied, "Rabbi, where are you staying?" "Come and see," Jesus said. And they did; they followed Jesus to his lodging place and stayed with him all through that day, questioning, listening, drawing upon the ceaseless depths that were in the Christ (John 1:35-42).

Then Andrew did something wonderfully characteristic of him: "He first found his brother Simon and said to him, 'We have found the Messiah'" (John 1:41). This is the Andrew who was a brother not simply in blood, but in spirit. Having found the Eternal Answer, the One for whom he had himself been seeking, Andrew first—*first!*—found his brother Simon to tell him the news.

Why do I think that's so significant and, as a matter of fact, wonderful? Because when we find a great thing our natural inclination is to sit and savor the excellence of it for a time, while we think of ways we can make more of what we have found. I'll concede that it ought really to be most natural of us to share our good fortune with those closest to us, but it doesn't always work that way. Sometimes, in fact, it's more difficult to be brotherly or sisterly with our relatives than with anyone else. Perhaps that would be especially true if your brother were a Simon Peter—a dynamic, vigorous person who so easily put you in the shade. I doubt that Andrew could remember many occasions in his life when the spotlight focused on him—and when it did, Simon probably adjusted the lens as quickly as possible. Not that Simon was a bad person; as a matter of fact, one could hardly keep from liking him. But he must some-times have become a little tiresome as a day-in, day-out brother. When people said to Andrew, "It must be fun to live around Simon," Andrew must sometimes have answered with mock excitement, "Yeah, a real ball. Just a load of laughs."

But Andrew was better than that. He *first* found his brother Simon, because he was a *brother*, a great-hearted soul who wanted, as soon as he had a good thing, to share it with some-one else. Especially with Simon!

And you know what happened next? Very shortly Simon Peter, the vociferous one, was part of the inner circle of three who were closest to Jesus. Then, with still more time, Simon was the foremost of the Twelve, always the first to speak, usu-ally the loudest, sometimes the erratic one, but nevertheless, the acknowledged leader of the group. As for Andrew, who had brought Simon Peter to Jesus, he was back in the crowd, taking his place as a supporting player.

I can't help wondering if Andrew ever got bitter over this development. I wonder if he said, "If it weren't for me, Simon would never have had a chance. *Now* look at him! He's the whole show, always having something to say." Andrew might have said that, and if he had, I, for one, would understand. But if I'm reading Andrew rightly, he would have answered my speculation with bewilderment. "*Resent* him? He's my *brother*."

John's Gospel tells a second story about Andrew, the brother (John 6:1-14). Five thousand people and more had followed Jesus into the wilderness, and now it was time to eat. Past time, in fact. Jesus asked Philip what should be done for the crowd, and Philip gave a sensible answer. It would take six months' wages, he said, to buy bread for a crowd like this.

Then Andrew made his contribution. "There's a boy here who has a lunch of five loaves and two fish." That was a stupid thing to say, wasn't it? Five loaves and two fish—enough to feed a boy, but an absurdity where an army of five thousand is waiting. So on further thought, Andrew added, apologetically, "But what are they among so many?"

It was like Andrew, of course, to notice the small boy. Your grandparents or great-grandparents had a phrase: "Children should be seen, and not heard." They talked that way in the first century, too. But Andrew was the kind of person a little boy could approach. While the other disciples were busy with bigger things, Andrew was chatting with a boy, patting him on the head, asking him where he had caught the fish—or did his mother buy them at market? A scruffy lad of no special promise, but Andrew—the brotherly type—visits with him and somewhat ridiculously thinks that his lunchbox will interest the Master.

Murillo, the seventeenth-century Spanish artist, painted a picture of Andrew suffering martyrdom on a cross. In his picture, Murillo has a little boy in the foreground, head turned away weeping, an arm across his eyes. I don't want to make too much of the matter, because Murillo liked to include children in his paintings; some critics have accused him of sentimentalism. But this is not a group of children, it's a boy, and I can't help thinking that Murillo is portraying the boy with the lunchbox, even if it is something of an anachronism to show him still as a boy years later.

The New Testament gives us just one more story about Andrew, and again it seems to me to be typical (John 12:20-22). Some Gentiles had come to Jerusalem at the time of the Passover, and they had heard about Jesus. They were curious, perhaps even hopeful. So they approached Philip, probably because he had a Gentile name, and they reasoned he might be their most likely point of entrance. So what did Philip do?

He went to Andrew. Why? I think it's because Andrew was a brother, a helpful human being, the kind of person you go to when there's an errand to be run, an appeal to be made, a cause to be furthered. So Andrew joined Philip in bringing the Gentiles to Jesus.

There you have the three New Testament stories about Andrew, the only stories the Bible tells of him with any specificity, and all from the Gospel of John. And in each one, he is being a brother to someone, because this is who he was: Andrew, a *brother*. And see how broad are his sympathies. In the first story he is brother to a relative, Simon. Sometimes, as I said, it's hard to be attentive to those close to us. Next, he's a brother to a little boy. Often it is easier to ignore those who are judged by our culture to be inconsequential. Finally, he is brother to the Gentiles. A person's sympathies must be very large to stretch arms around other nations, other races, and other social groups. Andrew was that kind of person.

Someone has said that Andrew was both the first home missionary and the first foreign missionary. He was a home missionary in the winning of his brother Simon, and a foreign missionary when he brought the Greeks to Jesus. We don't often use these designations in our day, but the point remains a valid one, and Andrew demonstrates it.

The New Testament tells us nothing more about Andrew, but tradition picks up the story just as it does for all of the disciples. This mass of tradition and legend should be viewed with a skeptical, and yet an appreciative, eye. According to fairly reliable tradition, Andrew preached in many lands, especially Scythia. In Andrew's time, "Scythian" was a synonym for any rough, uncouth, or savage person. Josephus said that the Scythians were "little different from wild beasts." It's appropriate, isn't it, that Andrew would be the missionary to the Scythians. He, the brotherly one, would reach out to this despised, apparently unattractive people.

And Scythia, as perhaps you know, is the country north of the Black Sea, between the River Danube and the River Tanais. That is, it is part of modern Russia. As a result, Andrew became known as the patron saint of Russia.

But because Andrew also preached in Greece, he became known as the patron saint of Greece. Furthermore, as golfers know, Andrew eventually became the patron saint of Scotland, and Scotland's greatest university is named for him. The Scots are proud of their Order of Saint Andrew, observing November 30, the traditional anniversary of Andrew's martyrdom, as their day of celebration.

Several years ago I looked up "Saint Andrew" in an urban telephone directory, that of Greater Cleveland, Ohio. I found in that area there were eight churches, an abbey, a church-related apartment building, and a neighborhood ministry that bore his name. The institutions ranged from Roman Catholic and a variety of Orthodox bodies to Baptist and Presbyterian. And as I've already indicated, Andrew has the rare distinction of being the patron saint for three countries. Not bad for a member of the crowd, a supporting actor!

It is said that Aegeas, governor of Patras in Greece, hated Andrew because Andrew had converted his wife and his brother to Christ, so he condemned Andrew to death. According to tradition, seven soldiers scourged Andrew with rods, then fastened him to a cross. It was an "X" type of cross, and is still known as a Saint Andrew's Cross. They did not nail him there, but sought to prolong his agony by binding him so that he would die slowly of hunger, thirst, and exposure.

Tradition further reports that Andrew suffered thus for several days, preaching to all who passed by, and praying. Legend says that his last words were, "Would, Father, that I had time to teach truth to my murderers. . . ."

So he died as he had lived, a brother. That's who he was: *Andrew, a brother.*

CHAPTER 2
PETER, MAN OF ACTION

READ MATTHEW 26:30-35, 69-75.

Simon Peter was a man of action. There was no predicting where the action might lead, but the action was guaranteed.

As a result, it's easy to find stories about Simon Peter. His was the kind of life that produced anecdotes. Let any four persons be involved in a given situation, with one of the four being Peter, and the stories that come out will center on Peter. If Peter had been a twenty-first-century athlete, it's at his locker that reporters would gather for a quote or a story. He was, as they say, "good press." Look at the passages in the four Gospels and the first twelve chapters of the book of Acts that tell of the apostles, and you'll find that some 60 percent focus in some measure on Simon Peter.

That's because Peter was always doing something. He was always in action. The action might be ridiculous or sublime, but there'd be action. While the others in the group were still pondering, Peter was usually speaking or doing.

Like several others of the apostles, Simon Peter was a fisherman. He made his home in Capernaum. Capernaum is a place you will almost surely visit if you make a trip to the Holy Land. The archaeological ruins in this area are among the most well documented. Jesus seems to have been especially well received in Capernaum; so much so, that when he returned to his hometown of Nazareth, the people said, "Do here also in your hometown the things that we have heard you did at

Capernaum" (Luke 4:23). So this city became the headquarters of Jesus' ministry in Galilee, and it is quite possible that Jesus worked out of Peter's house while he was in that region.

In the case of most of the apostles, we don't know whether or not they were married, although it is likely, because marriage was assumed as a way of life among the first-century Jewish people. But we have a definite record in Peter's case. The apostle Paul makes specific reference to Peter's marriage (1 Corinthians 9:5; NRSV refers to *Cephas*, Aramaic for "Rock," another name for Peter), and the Gospels tell of Jesus healing Peter's mother-in-law (Mark 1:30-31). We know nothing at all, however, about what Peter's wife was like; the Bible doesn't even give us her name. Perhaps that isn't too surprising, in light of Peter's dominant personality. A person was easily put in the shade when in Peter's presence.

He was a Galilean, and probably people of his day who lived in other places would have said that he was a very typical Galilean. Josephus, the historian, served for a time as governor of Galilee, so he knew Galileans well. He describes them as being notoriously quick in temper, and given to quarreling, but also the most chivalrous of men. Josephus also said, "They were ever fond of innovations, and by nature disposed to changes, and delighted in seditions. . . . They were ever ready to follow a leader and to begin an insurrection" (Josephus, *Wars of the Jews*, 3,3,2, and *Life*, 17, quoted in William Barclay, *The Master's Men*, Abingdon Press, 1959; page 18). Clearly enough, Peter was a true son of his province.

One of the best ways to catch the flavor and personality of Peter is to read the Gospel of Mark—perhaps especially to read it aloud. Scholars have agreed since earliest times (indeed, beginning with Papias, Bishop of Hierapolis, in the first half of the second century) that Mark was Peter's interpreter, and that his Gospel is hardly other than a recording of the preaching and personality of Peter.

We get the impetuous, active Peter in the very way the Gospel of Mark begins—not with the story of the infancy or birth of Jesus, but with the ministry of John the Baptist as he set out to prepare the way for Jesus. Mark plunges us full-depth into the story of Jesus at the very point where Peter himself is called to follow Jesus. Dr. Edward George once suggested that if we would cast the opening chapters of Mark in the first person, we might almost hear Peter talking. We're often reminded that the most characteristic word in Mark's Gospel is the Greek word *euthus*, which is translated "straightway" or "immediately." I can't imagine a word that would be more characteristic of Simon Peter, the man of action.

Needless to say, someone who is quick to act is inevitably susceptible to many errors. If you know anything about Simon Peter, you know that he had his full share. One might expect that the Gospel of Mark might eliminate or at least play down some of the incidents that portray Peter in less than favorable light. No so. Mark's Gospel offers Peter in full color, in his occasional heroism and his more notable stumblings.

Whatever Simon Peter did, he did with a flourish. As I noted in the opening chapter, Peter was introduced to Jesus by his brother, Andrew. But Peter was very soon a member of the little group of three that was closest to Jesus, and soon after that he was spokesman for the whole group of Jesus' disciples.

One day Jesus took Peter, James, and John—the inner circle—with him to a secluded mountain place. While they were there, they had a remarkable experience. Jesus was suddenly transfigured before them, taking on a nonearthly appearance, and they saw Elijah and Moses conversing with him. The experience was overpowering. James and John stood in awestruck silence.

Not Peter. He blurted, "Rabbi, it is good for us to be here; let us make three dwellings, one for you, one for Moses, and one for Elijah" (Mark 9:5). The Gospel writer is kind enough to make an excuse for Peter: "He did not know what to say" (verse 6). Some people are silent when they don't know what to say. Peter was the kind who felt obligated to say something, even if it happened to be the wrong thing. And of course that's one of the reasons he appeals to us so much. When we see him in such self-revealing moments, we recognize him as our kin, and we like him for it.

One of the highest moments in Peter's life—indeed, probably the very highest—occurred when Jesus asked his disciples what people were saying about him. After receiving their varied reports, Jesus turned the question to its crucial form: "Who do *you* say that I am?" And of course it was Simon Peter who answered: "You are the Messiah, the Son of the living God" (Matthew 16:16). In that moment of impetuous inspiration, Peter gave the church its basic creedal statement; in one impulsive sentence, he summed up the doctrine of Christianity. On the rock of that confession, the church stands or falls.

But as surely as Peter set the future course of the church in that awesome moment, within perhaps the same hour he previewed our frequent failures. Because of Peter's declaration of faith, Jesus began to pledge the disciples to secrecy, warning them that he would soon be taken prisoner, tried, and killed; and on the third day, he would rise again. Peter bristled at the thought of his Lord suffering. "God forbid it, Lord!" he said. "This must never happen to you" (Matthew 16:22).

Peter meant well, but he was so wrong. He wanted desperately to save Jesus from hurt and harm, not realizing that the fulfillment of Jesus' calling was by this very route of suffering and crucifixion. Peter, with all of his good intentions, was setting out to sabotage the issue of Jesus' calling. So Jesus turned on him, speaking as vigorously in reproof as before he had spoken in praise. "Get behind me, Satan! You are a stumbling block to me; for you are setting your mind not on divine things but on human things" (verse 23). I see Peter falling back into the tail of the procession, ashamed, hurt, bewildered, perhaps even resentful. He bites his tongue in disgust with himself, yet is probably still convinced in his own mind that his counsel is right.

And of course we continue in Peter's style. We are always trying to reroute the way of the cross into a path of comfort, of superficial achievement, of frothy popularity.

In the last hours before the Crucifixion, Peter rose to heights and plunged to depths in a wild roller coaster of emotions. At the meal we now call the Last Supper, Jesus set out to wash the feet of the disciples—an assignment ordinarily fulfilled by slaves. Peter reacted with horror. "You'll never wash my feet!" But when Jesus answered, "If I don't wash your feet, you have no part in me," Peter hurtled to the other extreme: "Not only my feet, Lord, but also my head and my hands" (see John 13:1-20).

During the course of the meal, Jesus warned the disciples that all of them would forsake him. Again, Peter—with fine disregard for the feelings of his comrades—contradicted his Lord. "Even though all become deserters, I will not" (Mark 14:29). Nor was Peter deterred when Jesus singled him out with a further, more specific warning. "Even though I must die with you, I will not deny you," Peter said. Emboldened by Peter's vigor, "all of them said the same" (Mark 14:31). And all of them, of course, were wrong, and no one more dramatically so than Peter.

You remember what happened. As Jesus stood in trial before Caiaphas, Peter watched from out at the edge of the courtyard. Within a brief period, Peter was asked three times if he were not a follower of Jesus, and three times he denied it—at last doing so with a violent oath. So, again, Peter was heroic one minute and cowardly the next. So well-meaning, so consumed by good intentions, but so terribly, terribly human.

They crucified Jesus and laid him in a tomb. Once again, Peter was the man of action. Early in the morning of the third day, Peter and John went to the tomb. On the way, they met Mary Magdalene, who told them the tomb was empty. Peter and John began to run, and because John was the younger, he arrived at the tomb first. But he stood outside; perhaps it was the caution of love, or perhaps a fear of seeing the swathed body of his Lord. Not Peter. When he got to the tomb, he did just what you would expect him to do: He charged directly in (John 20:1-10).

For the next number of weeks, Jesus visited his followers at unpredictable intervals, then left them entirely on their own. With Jesus gone, Peter emerged more than ever as the major spokesman, although the actual administrative leader of the early Christian church seems to have been James, a younger brother of Jesus. On the Day of Pentecost, it was Peter who stood up to address the crowd and to lead the first great ingathering of souls. Peter was the leader—by temperament, by ability, and by the ready acquiescence of his colleagues.

It was only a matter of time until the early church faced a major crisis: To what degree should the church accept Gentiles into the body of believers? Again, Peter was all Peter, acting without hesitancy, then reversing his stand. It was Peter who at first pleaded effectively for the Gentiles to be admitted to the church, for Peter had received a vision declaring that God could make even the Gentiles clean and acceptable. But a little later, as Paul points out in the letter to the Galatians, Peter shifted his ground and turned his back on the newcomers, until Paul himself shamed Peter into defending them (Acts 11:1-18; Galatians 2:11-16).

The Bible tells us very little more about Peter's activities, because midway in the book of Acts, Paul becomes the major personality. But of course tradition and legend have preserved scores, perhaps hundreds, of stories about Peter. Some of them are no doubt true, and others just as surely are exaggerations or unreliable tales.

Perhaps the best remembered and most appealing story has to do with Peter's preaching in Rome. There, as the story recalls, he met frightening opposition, until at last he felt his life was in danger. Peter's friends urged him to flee, so that his life might be spared. It was a reasonable suggestion; after all, consider how much good he could do if his life were spared.

But as Peter was leaving Rome, according to the legend, he saw his Lord coming into the city. "*Domine, quo vadis?*" Peter asked: "Lord, whither goest thou?"

"I go to be crucified."

"Lord, art thou being crucified again?"

"Yes, Peter, I am being crucified again" (Barclay, *The Master's Men*, 26, quoting the apocryphal Acts of Peter, 35).

Peter realized that Jesus was going to Rome to bear the cross from which he was fleeing. The great fisherman returned to the city. Tradition says that the officials first crucified Peter's wife, forcing him to look on. Peter faced his death with such courage that his jailer was won to the Christian faith. When the time came for Peter's own execution, he insisted on being crucified with his head down, declaring that he was not worthy to die as his Lord had died.

Thus, heroically, did he die, the Galilean fisherman from Capernaum who blessed humanity with the passion of his faith. Hundreds of millions of Roman Catholics around the world hold him in unique reverence, looking upon him as the first leader of the church. But every Christian, of whatever denomination, must rightly hold Peter in regard and remember him with gratitude.

He was a man of action. He wasn't always right, but he was never disqualified for not trying. I think he would have been driven to distraction by our present pattern of doing things by way of committee meetings, long-range plans, and flowcharts.

I'm not sure that he would fit into any of our major denominations, Catholic or Protestant, if he were among us today. A bishop, of whatever church, might be inclined to appoint Peter to the farthest corner of the judicatory area, so he wouldn't see him more than once a year.

Committees are a good thing, mind you, and so too is proper deliberation. As a person who has had his ministry in a highly structured system, I'm quick to say that it has been good for me. My mistakes would have been multiplied if it weren't for such restraints. Nor can anyone rightly defend all of Peter's rashness and impetuosity. But if rashness sometimes leads to sins of commission, overdeliberation leads to sins of omission. I know where Peter's sins would have been. What would he say of ours?

So here's to Saint Peter. We probably like him better as a historical figure than we would as a contemporary coworker. But we need him. When the last committee has filed its weary report, and the last long-range study has been put somewhere to gather dust, we will still need our Simon Peters: men and women of action, fire, and holy love.

CHAPTER 3
$\mathscr{J}$AMES,
UNFULFILLED LEADER

READ MARK 10:35-45.

Simple logic says that James, the son of Zebedee, ought to be remembered as one of the greatest of the original Twelve. Just as we remember the exploits of Peter and the sharply etched personality of John, we should have vivid pictures and memories of James, because James belongs with Peter and John. Instead, however, any picture we have of James is a relatively obscure one.

James was a Galilean, son of Zebedee and brother of John—the same John who became known as "the beloved disciple." James probably lived in Bethsaida Julias, which was a rapidly growing provincial capital and also a great center for the fishing business. In fact, Bethsaida's significance for the industry is demonstrated by its very name: *Bethsaida* means "house of fish."

So we're not surprised that James was a fisherman. He was associated in business with his brother John, his father, Zebedee, and perhaps in some way with another pair of brothers, Simon and Andrew. James was part of what was, for its time, a rather large-scale enterprise. He and his partners ran a kind of wholesale business, engaging in deep-water fishing. This kind of fishing called for larger boats and heavier nets (and thus, a larger capital investment), and a good-sized, able crew. Zebedee, the father of James and John, was enough of an entrepreneur to keep several hired hands as part of his crew, along with his sons (Mark 1:19-20).

So James was part of a thriving business, and probably heir to a modest bit of money. But like the other young fishermen in his circle, he hungered for something more than success and creature comforts. I think all of us have such longings, but a good many of us allow these feelings to be pushed aside by the insistent voices of our culture and its demands. Yes, and by logic, too; after all, ought not one take care for tomorrow, to build up the traditional nest egg?

But not James. The immediate was not enough. When he heard of the wilderness preacher, John the Baptist, tradition says that James went out to hear him, as did several of his friends. And when the wilderness prophet called for repentance and baptism, James was one of the persons who stepped forward for immersion and all that it promised of a deeper walk with God.

We are sometimes critical of persons who wander from church to church. And perhaps with reason, because such wandering may be a sign of instability, and of an unreadiness to put down roots and assume continuing responsibilities. But it may also be a sign of a very authentic heart-hunger. This certainly was the case with James, John, Andrew, and Simon Peter. Raised in the mainstream of Judaism, they were at first drawn to the prophetic voice of John the Baptist; then, when Jesus appeared, they were quick to follow him. A person who is on the quest may stop at several way stations before finding what the heart desires. But being on a pilgrimage toward God is never reason for apology; at least, not as long as we're wanting our quest to lead to a destination and a commitment.

So James left his fishing nets and his successful business, with the measure of security it offered, in order to follow the new teacher, Jesus of Nazareth. Almost immediately he became part of the inner circle, a group of three who were closest to Jesus and on whom Jesus seemed especially to rely.

The New Testament reports three occasions when Jesus

took this small group aside. Once it was during a time of special need, the visit to Jairus's daughter. The atmosphere at this scene was redolent with unbelief—an unbelief that, in fact, bordered on scorn. Jesus shut out everyone except these three men and the child's parents. The second occasion was the event we refer to as the Transfiguration (mentioned briefly in the last chapter), when Jesus was bathed in light and was seen conversing with Elijah and Moses. The third was the crucial hour of prayer in Gethsemane, hours before Jesus' trial and crucifixion. It was these same three persons who Jesus asked to stand watch with him while he struggled with the prospects and terrors that lay just ahead. In each of these key instances, the inner group was composed of Peter, James, and John.

Here's where our story takes its strange turn. We know all about Peter, of course. There's no question he fulfilled the leadership role that was expected of him. We know almost as much about John, the beloved disciple. His name and his story are familiar to us, leaving no doubt but that he became the great Christian leader we expected him to be. But what happened to James, the third member of the inner circle, the older brother of John and the one who might therefore be expected to show even more fulfillment? It appears that Jesus judged him to be as promising as Peter and John, yet most of us know very little of him. What happened to James, whose promise of leadership seems to have been so great?

One thing is sure, James was *willing* to be a leader. Jesus gave a nickname to James and his brother John after they had joined his band of disciples: "Sons of Thunder," he called them (Mark 3:17). We'll talk more about that title when we paint John's picture, but let's pause long enough to see the obvious implications in the title, since it belongs to James as well as John. I think Jesus used the term playfully, but to make a point. It seems clear that he recognized the temperament of these two brothers and put a friendly tag on them that would remind them of the incendiary quality of their natures. "Sons of thunder": loud, rumbling, sometimes threatening and about to burst. This is the kind of person James was, along with his brother, John. The potential of a leader was surely there, if someone could only channel all the thunder and bombast into productive efforts.

The Gospels tell us two stories in which James plays a special part, and the thunder can be heard in both. The two events happened during the last weeks of Jesus' life, after the disciples had been under the Master's influence for several years, so they could be expected to know the spirit of their Lord. Yet watch James.

Jesus and the disciples were headed toward Jerusalem, the last trip Jesus would make to the beloved city. They sent messengers ahead to a village in Samaria to make the way ready for the Master. Probably the disciples were upset that Jesus wanted anything to do with the Samaritans, because the feeling between Jews and Samaritans was bad, and had been for roughly six centuries. Nevertheless, they probably weren't ready for the reply they received. The Samaritans simply refused Jesus' request. If he were going to Jerusalem, it wouldn't be through their territory.

Now it's one thing for me to look on you with impatient disdain, but it's quite another when you show the same feelings toward me. And it's all the worse if I have extended some gesture of friendliness to you, however half-hearted or insincere it might be. Probably all the disciples felt some indignation, but no one as much as James and John. When they heard the report, they did what came most naturally to them. They thundered. Yes, and a little lightning, too. "Lord," they said, "do you want us to command fire to come down from heaven and consume them?" (Luke 9:54).

That's our James! If people won't cooperate with you, wipe them out! Does the committee disagree with you? Disband the committee, and appoint a new one. Has the organization voted contrary to your desires? Pronounce an anathema on them, and quit. Show them they can't treat *you* that way! To be honest, most of us understand James in this scene, because most of us have had some occasions in our lives when we've felt the same way. Not to the point, probably, of calling down fire from heaven, but we've had some pretty scorching thoughts.

In my youth, I knew a preacher like James. He had been a small-time boxer when he was young, and he'd never quite gotten over it. Some Sundays when he was tirading against sin in our community, he would pause, posture a bit, and say, "What those fellows need is for someone to beat them within an inch of their lives—and I'm just the fellow who could do it." Such a statement always had a wonderfully electrifying effect on the more combative saints.

But as I said a moment ago, there's a little of James in most of us. There are people who feel that the best way to handle most international problems would be to drop an occasional atomic bomb. And, sadly, there are parents whose first response to their children is a blow to the side of the head. And of course you'll find some civilized descendants of James in action in many committee discussions or public debates. These are the people who quickly leave the realm of fact and logic, and resort to sarcasm and innuendo. Logicians have a name for one aspect of this approach: *ad hominem*, or trying to destroy the person's case, not by answering his argument, but by attacking his character.

Not much further along in the story, as the apostles and Jesus were drawing near to Jerusalem, James and John took Jesus aside for a private conversation. Apparently they felt that Jesus was coming to Jerusalem to set up his kingdom, so they were thinking ahead. "Teacher, we want you to do for us whatever we ask of you." Jesus urged them to make their request known. "Grant us to sit, one at your right hand and one at your left, in your glory" (Mark 10:35-37).

Our first reaction, when we listen in on this conversation, is to marvel at the audacity of these two brothers. But on further thought, we realize that James and John had some basis for making their request. After all, they were part of the inner circle, along with Simon Peter, so they had reason to think that some primary role of leadership should come to them. But obviously, they didn't want to leave it to chance—nor even, come to think of it, to the unaided judgment of Jesus. They were confident that Jesus would soon ascend to a throne, and when he did, they wanted to be sure that one of the two of them was in line for the prime minister's post, and that the other was named chancellor of the exchequer. James and John may have been short on modesty and on consideration for their colleagues, but nobody can say that they lacked ambition!

Another factor also comes to mind as we watch this scene. By this time the opposition to Jesus was building to a point where it looked as if he were heading inevitably toward destruction. The rumblings of doom were growing more menacing by the hour. I'm not sure whether James and John had such faith that they could look the mounting data in the eye and still think the Kingdom was on the way, or whether they were simply so enamored of their own ambitions that they couldn't see the cross that lay just ahead. In any event, they presented their case to the Master.

Jesus treated their request with surprising kindness. Perhaps he saw beneath their apparent arrogance the elements of character that would someday make for greatness. The other disciples, however, became indignant. Jesus turned the painful scene into a teaching moment, pleading with his errant band for sacrificial service.

In any event, it's clear that James was cut out to be a leader, and that he very much wanted to be one. The son of a rather successful businessman, chosen for the inner circle of Jesus' disciples and possessed of explosive vigor and ambition, he seemed a prime candidate for leadership.

But while Peter and John, the other parties in the three-some, went on to their predicted achievements, James's story came to a premature conclusion. In A.D. 42, King Herod launched a new persecution of the Christian church. He arrested several of the disciples, then killed James, making him the first martyr from among the original Twelve (Acts 12:1-2). (Stephen, of course, was the very first Christian martyr, but James was the first of the apostles so to die.)

So it is that James's leadership potential was never really fulfilled. Most of us want to raise a typical question: What might James have become if he had been allowed to live a few years longer? Why must the life of so capable a person be cut short? We are likely to see James as a tragic figure, a person of superior potential who never had the opportunity to bring his possibilities to their farthest reach.

But when I identify James by the phrase "Unfulfilled Leader," I do so in the language of secular judgment, not by the insight of faith nor of eternity. And *eternity* ought, for you and me, to be the final measure of success, and of all other judgments.

The Bible does not tell us any specifics about James's death, but tradition—particularly through the writings of Clement of Alexandria—leaves a likely account. According to this ancient report, a man named Josias brought the accusation against James that caused his condemnation. But when Josias saw the faith and character with which James conducted himself in his final hours, even in the face of betrayal and death, he was so moved that he declared himself a Christian.

So James and Josias were led away together to be beheaded. On the way, Josias begged James to forgive him. James paused, then said, "Peace be with you," and he kissed the man who had betrayed him. The two men were then beheaded at the same time. When in our contemporary liturgy we engage in the passing of the peace, perhaps we will feel a more profound content in that phrase when we contemplate the James-Josias scene.

If I may say so, in this hour of death, James was a leader in the most important of all enterprises—the leading of another person to our Lord, and from there, to victorious death. And in a sense (a strange, wonderful, and ultimate sense), James did come to sit at his Lord's right hand in the Kingdom. For the only throne to which Jesus came on this earth was the throne of a cross—a cross that bore a sign describing Jesus as "King of the Jews"—and as we noted earlier, James was the first of the Twelve to follow his Lord to the place of death for the faith. And when James died, he did so in the style of his Master, praying forgiveness for the very persons responsible for his death.

If you will look at that Calvary scene with the careful eyes of faith, you will see that the cross on which our Lord is lifted up is, in the eternal sense, a throne; for it is here that Jesus Christ won the eternal battle for our human race. Now stretch your faith with some holy imagination. Remember that disciple who wanted, in the kingdom, to be at Jesus' right or left hand? Does he seem to be in that place, as the first of the disciples to die for the faith?

There are ways and ways to measure leadership. Standards of judgment are not the same for poets and halfbacks, for executives and Sisters of Charity. So how shall we judge whether James, the fisherman, the volatile son of thunder, was fulfilled as a leader? Ponder this, that he finished his work, and that he was faithful to the end. And consider that he led the way, for the little original band, into the path of ultimate sacrifice, of martyrdom. I think that's a bit of leading—in fact, leading of such proportions that not many of us easily feel qualified to follow.

One thing more. According to a legend, in A.D. 813 the grave of James was discovered in an obscure corner of north-eastern Spain. The place was named *Santiago de Compostela* (Santiago is Spanish for "James"), and it is now the site of a Roman Catholic cathedral and a key destination for pilgrimages; for a time in the Middle Ages, it was third only to Rome and Jerusalem, and it is still the destination of the 484-mile French Pilgrims' Road, the Camino de Santiago. So it is, that devout pilgrims of many stripes still find James as their leader.

So we hear James's thunder still. It is the thunder of redeeming love, leading us—if we will—to higher ground.

CHAPTER 4
*P*HILIP, THE DELIBERATE

READ JOHN 1:43-48.

If you want to understand the apostle named Philip, you might best start with his name. Names are often revealing. At the least, they say something about our parents—their affections, dreams, and loyalties. Some names reflect ethnic ties, while others strive almost ludicrously to avoid them. A child's name often shows the strength of family bonds, as when a baby is named for a parent or relative, or is given a paternal or maternal family name. In still other cases, names reveal the longings of a parent, so that a family of modest means gives a child a name as if they were to the manor born, or shy parents tag a child with a name that sounds as if it were chosen by a public relations firm. As one who reads the sports section, I expect that someday someone will write a dissertation on the names of quarterbacks in the National Football League—and what part the names played in developing the qualities that get a young man into such a role of leadership.

So look at *Philip*. As you and I see it, his name seems sound and acceptable enough, with no particular significance. But it must have raised eyebrows when his parents gave it to him. Philip was a Jew, born in Bethsaida on the Sea of Galilee, but his name is a Greek name. Again, that probably doesn't startle you or me, but I'm sure it was shocking in that first-century world where barriers between Jews and Gentiles were so formidable. I venture that when Philip was brought to the

Temple for his first presentation, some of the more pious and orthodox whispered, "But why a *Greek* name? Why didn't his father choose one of the great names of our own people?"

And frankly, that's a good question. Of course we can't know for sure why Philip's parents gave him a Greek name. It could be simply that one of his parents was Greek. But some observers have come up with a more likely reason. Philip's birthplace, Bethsaida, was for many years little more than a sleepy fishing village. Then a man named Philip became tetrarch of Ituraea—something like a provincial governor. This Philip was the best of the sons of Herod, and he enjoyed a long and peaceful reign. In the course of his governing, he made Bethsaida the capital of the province. With this, the village gained a number of impressive public buildings and a substantial increase in population—and with it all, some prosperity. It could well be, therefore, that Philip's father named his son Philip in honor of the governor who had brought so many benefits to the area. It's even possible that Philip's father was tied to the governor in some modest political ways that made him feel indebted.

In any event, Philip grew up in a much more cosmopolitan setting than was experienced by the other apostles. I think it's fair to assume that his home would have been open to new ideas. Very possibly it was a meeting place for people of other nationalities and cultures; his Greek name implies as much. But it must also have had substantial Jewish commitments, because when Philip came to manhood, he affiliated himself—as did Andrew, Peter, James, and John—with the new preacher of righteousness, John the Baptist.

The first three Gospels, Matthew, Mark, and Luke, tell us nothing about Philip. In those Gospels he is only a name in the listing of the Twelve. As with Andrew, it is John's Gospel that saves Philip from oblivion. In truth, it probably would have been easy for Philip to have been lost in the shadows, for he seems to have been a retiring sort of person. He appears four times in John's Gospel, and in three of the four stories, someone is seeking *him*; only once is he the initiator of a relationship.

That may cause some of us to find encouragement in Philip. People sometimes feel that only certain kinds of personalities become vigorously involved in the faith enterprises. They look at those of us who are caught up in our faith, and say, sometimes sadly, "I wish I could be like that, but it's just not my temperament. You know, I'm not very emotional. I'm private about religion, and sort of matter-of-fact. You can count on my being in church and supporting it, but I guess I'll never be a saint. I'm just not that mystical."

Well, our best evidence indicates that Philip was of just such a temperament. He was the deliberate one: matter-of-fact, retiring, perhaps a little shy. Someone has called him "prosaic" and with good reason. Yet Jesus chose him as one of the Twelve, because he saw in Philip some of the qualities his company needed. It may well have been Philip's very matter-of-factness that made him attractive.

Let me tell you the four stories where Philip played a part. The first is from a day in Galilee when Jesus first met him. Jesus said, "Follow me." The Gospel doesn't say whether Philip followed Jesus immediately, or not. It reports, rather, that he in turn found Nathanael, and said to him, "We have found him about whom Moses in the law and also the prophets wrote, Jesus son of Joseph from Nazareth" (John 1:45).

There you have it: Philip, the deliberate one. His statement is as plain as you might find in a math textbook, as detailed as an analysis in a doctoral dissertation, and as awkward and uninspiring as a sentence can be. "We have found him about whom Moses in the law and also the prophets wrote, Jesus son of Joseph from Nazareth."

You see, Philip would not simply report that Moses had foretold Jesus; he had to be more detailed and exact: "Moses in the law." This is the kind of wordiness that would drive a copy editor to despair. I can see one blue-penciling the phrase as he or she shouts, "Where under heaven would Moses speak of anything but 'in the law'?" *All* of Moses' writings were classified as "the Law."

Nor was Philip satisfied to stop with the name of Jesus; he went on to tell the town from which Jesus had come, and his family descent. This was a deliberate man. You greeted him in the morning with a conventional "How are you?" and he would reply with remarks about his pulse, his temperature, his blood pressure, and a report on some recent X-rays.

If you think I'm overdoing it, compare Philip's story with that of Andrew, which is reported only a paragraph earlier in John's Gospel. Andrew met Jesus, and he too wanted to tell someone else. But when he came to Simon with the news, he said it this way: "We have found the Messiah!" (see John 1:40-41). You want to punctuate Andrew's report with exclamation points; Philip's calls for a full complement of commas and semicolons.

When we think of evangelism, we usually think of the Andrew style. We picture a person all ablaze, who talks with staccato excitement, abounding in exclamations and perhaps also in near-hyperboles. But believe me, there is also a place for the Philips, those persons who carefully and precisely tell their story. In the twenty-first-century world of advertising, Philip would be the apostle of the "soft sell." But let's admit that both Andrew and Philip are needed—both the exclamatory enthusiasm of Andrew and the cautious precision of Philip.

The next time we meet Philip, Jesus is faced with five thousand who have followed him into the wilderness, and who need now to be fed. You will remember that Jesus looked over the great, milling throng, then turned to Philip with a question: "Where are we to buy bread for these people to eat?" (John 6:5). The Gospel writer tells us that Jesus asked this question to test Philip. Well, Jesus picked the right one. Philip wouldn't give a pious answer, such as "Everything is possible for you," nor would he be the professional pessimist: "Let's just get out of here as soon as possible." Philip the deliberate got out his mental "calculator" to give his reasoned answer: "Six months' wages would not buy enough bread for each of them to get a little" (John 6:7).

Someone has said that Philip was a person with a warm heart and a pessimistic head. When I think back on my nearly forty years as a pastor, I realize that I've known a variety of Philips. They really, sincerely want to do something for others, but they can't see how it can ever be done. This is the particular problem of the deliberate: They ponder so long on the problems of their course that they can easily be paralyzed into inaction.

But on the other hand, a good word needs to be said for Philip and his kind. Granted that in this case Jesus fed the five thousand through a miracle; and granted that Andrew was the hero of this story as he brought forward the little boy with the loaves and fish. But in the daily run of life, miracles are few. The thousands are usually fed by just such prosaic methods as Philip offered. Now and then, manna falls from heaven, and we never tire (nor should we) of telling the story of such miracles. But most of the time we need a Philip, one who will wet the stub of his pencil and calculate on the back of an envelope until the building is paid for or the budget raised or the food sent to India. Philip the deliberate: Sometimes he looks foolish because of his hesitancy, but often we need his sturdy practicality. I want some Philips in my church. Not too many, but a good sprinkling.

Then there was a day when a group of Greeks came searching for Jesus. As I said earlier, they did a logical thing: They approached Jesus through the disciple with a Greek name, no doubt reasoning that either he was Greek or that he would have Greek sympathies.

So what did Philip do? Just what you might expect a person of his natural conservatism to do. Perhaps it was because he wasn't sure that it was proper to bring persons of another nation and culture to Jesus, or perhaps it was simply his natural inclination to confer with a colleague, to do "further research," as we say in the academic world. Whatever Philip did, he did cautiously. So instead of going directly to Jesus, Philip took the men to Andrew, apparently to see what Andrew would recommend. After all, if you're Philip, there's nothing like getting a second opinion. And of course Andrew did just what you would expect Andrew to do; he took the men directly to the Master.

It's pretty much the same scenario as was played out in the feeding of the five thousand. I don't think Philip was unwilling to feed the multitudes, nor to bring outsiders to Jesus; it's just that he was very deliberate. But always note this, that while he was deliberate, he was not an obstructionist. When Jesus began to use the boy's loaves and fish, Philip didn't get in the way, nor did he hinder Andrew as he took the Greeks to Jesus. When others moved, Philip readily moved with them. To be deliberate should not mean to be negative, though I think some try to excuse their negativism and their unwillingness to move by insisting that they simply want time to think. When you hear someone make a motion to send something back to a committee for further study, it's sometimes hard to know if it's Philip, the deliberate, talking, or Henry (or Sally or Bill), the obstructionist.

Here's the measure of Philip's integrity. When the Greeks came to him, he went to a person who was likely to be both understanding and aggressive. So while he may not have had the faith or the outgoing nature to go directly to Jesus, he did have the sense to seek help from someone who might have the gifts that he lacked.

And then there's the final discussion between Jesus and his disciples, a discussion that covers several chapters in the Gospel of John. Basically, it's an extended heart-sharing by our Lord, but on several occasions one disciple or another raises a question. Early in the presentation, Jesus said, "No one comes to the Father except through me. If you know me, you will know my Father also." Philip, ever on the search for more data, asked, "Lord, show us the Father, and we will be satisfied" (John 14:6-8).

There's nothing wrong with what Philip said. And believe me, it's consistent with who he was. Philip always wanted as much information as possible; he always insisted on adequate research. I don't think it was unbelief, in the style of Thomas, when he missed an early Resurrection appearance; it was only that Philip needed to know more.

Philip's request opened the door for one of Jesus' most stirring statements—one, in fact, that is crucial to our grasp of Christian doctrine. "Whoever has seen me," Jesus said, "has seen the Father" (John 14:9). If we want to know what God is like, we need only to look at Jesus Christ. How many times have you heard someone say, "I believe in the God of Jesus Christ" or "I know what God is like, because I know what Jesus is like"? These statements have their source in the whole gospel story, but the succinct summing-up of that story comes to us through the dialogue between Jesus and Philip. By Philip's very hesitancy, he provided us with a new legacy of understanding.

The New Testament tells us nothing more about Philip. One of the leading personalities in the book of Acts is named Philip, but he is a deacon in the church at Jerusalem rather than Philip the apostle. Tradition has a generous collection of extravagant legends about Philip, but most of them are so fantastic that there's no real value in repeating them. Even the story of his death is too shrouded in legend to be of much worth. We know only, with some certainty, that Philip became one of the great missionary preachers of Asia, and that he was martyred at Hierapolis.

But back to his name. Remember how we said his father had probably named him after the governor of Ituraea? Today, the Western world counts Philip as one of its perennially popular names, rising and falling with the tides of favor, but always present.

And why do you think this name keeps reappearing? Is it in honor of that ancient, provincial governor of Ituraea? Or is it perhaps because of the father of Alexander the Great?

Hardly! The governor of Ituraea is long forgotten. Even the father of Alexander the Great, though significant as a powerful ruler, is known today only by those who pay attention to ancient Greek or Roman history. We name our sons Philip, and our daughters Phyllis, not after Philip of Ituraea, but indirectly, through a long line of faith, after Philip, the fisherman of Bethsaida.

No doubt the quiet Galilean fisherman held Governor Philip in awe, but it is his name that has left a mark throughout our culture. He wasn't a man who bowled one over, never compelling in his enthusiasm, but he found his place in the sacred company of the apostles. Call him Philip the deliberate—and rejoice in the fact that our Lord has need and work for every temperament and every personality. Let the church rejoice in its wonderful, sometimes frustrating, human variety!

Chapter 5
James the Less

READ MARK 15:33-41.

I want to nominate the disciple called James the Less—the son of Alphaeus and Mary—as the Apostle of All the World's Forgotten People.

This will guarantee him quite a following, you know. Andy Warhol (perhaps a dubious authority) promised that "in the future everyone will be famous for fifteen minutes." But even if Warhol proves right, that leaves many of us with a vast desert of time when we will be quite unnoticed.

In truth, almost all of us feel on some days that life is passing us by, and that no one is deeply concerned that this is so. And some people, God bless them, feel this way most of their lives. In some cases, these feelings are with reason, because life seems to deal a dull hand to some people. In other instances, we wonder why the person feels so bereft, because on the surface, his or her life is not all that bad. But the measure is not sheer logic and data. One's life is not simply what the facts prove it to be, but what one perceives it to be. For all those persons who—correctly or not, and for whatever length of time—feel themselves forgotten, I bring you James the Less.

We usually assume that all the apostles were notable figures. Not always good, necessarily, and not always wise, but always outstanding. We recall that Jesus chose only twelve, and we reason that since he was working with such a small number, all of them must have been remarkable people. Besides, there's an inevitable aura of glamour about these men. Our churches memorialize them with stained glass windows, and we enshrine their memory with ancient symbols. Indeed, the New Testament book of Revelation tells us that the walls of the heavenly city will have twelve foundations bearing their names (Revelation 21:14). That ought to pretty well settle the question of greatness.

And it is easy to make such a case when you're speaking of Peter, James, John, and Matthew, or even of such a controversial figure as Thomas; indeed, even Judas, the betrayer, is a strikingly memorable figure, although a tragic one. But what do you do with someone like James the Less? Here is the apostle about whom we know the least, a figure lost in the deadening shadows of obscurity. And furthermore, his name seems to authorize such a role.

The Bible tells us so little about James the Less that we might sum it up in a paragraph. His name is mentioned only five times, and each time it is only as part of a list. James always appears in the listing of the apostles, but nothing further is ever said of him. Mark's Gospel mentions him in the Crucifixion story, but again, it is only as a name among names.

We do learn from Mark's reference, however, that James the Less probably came from a devout home, several or all of whom were followers of Jesus Christ. We read that when Jesus was crucified, several women stood at a distance looking on, including Mary Magdalene and Mary the mother of James the Less (also known as James the Younger); and we're told that these women had followed Jesus when he was in Galilee and had "ministered to him" there. So we know this much about James, that he had the benefit of a godly home and a mother who was devoted to Jesus. In this he was fortunate, fortunate to the utmost, because a child can receive no greater gift from parents than the gift of influence toward a living faith in Christ.

Let me interject at this moment an observation about the irony of life as many people (perhaps most) know it in the Western world. So many work so admirably to give their children every "advantage": a lovely home and yard, complete with swing set and recreation room; instruction in some musical instrument, dance, ballet; a trust fund to guarantee their getting a college education. And then—well, then, in so many cases, we let the soul go hang. But what shall it profit children if they receive vitamin D and niacin, piano lessons and a superb education, if they lose their own souls? Or what shall a child give in exchange for a home where Jesus Christ is Lord?

So whatever else James may not have had, he had this: a mother who followed Christ, and a father of the same conviction. And having this, he was a fortunate human being.

But the Bible tells us nothing more about him. We don't know, for example, how he came to follow Jesus. Some of the disciples have striking conversion stories, or at least stories that merited recording. We know that Matthew was sitting at his tax collector's booth when Jesus called him, and that he rose up and left his business to follow his Lord. And we know about Nathanael, whose call came with a peculiar quality of mysticism and awe. And of course we know, later, the dramatic story of Saul of Tarsus, who was struck from his horse, temporarily blinded, and engaged by a voice from heaven. And for that matter, even the unnamed Ethiopian eunuch in the book of Acts is remembered for an extraordinary conversion.

But not all conversions are so memorable. They may be to the subject of the event, but not necessarily to anyone else. The New Testament calls conversion the "new birth," and the birth analogy is an apt one. As surely as some babies come to birth with a measure of difficulty and drama, just so some persons go through a difficult process of spiritual birth. In physical birth, on the other hand, a doctor sometimes acknowl-edges to himself, as he or she leaves the delivery room, that the delivery would probably have taken place just as easily with no doctor present; so, too, some people are born into the kingdom of God so simply that the pastor and the Sunday school teacher feel they have done little to bring the event to pass. Indeed, they may not even have been conscious that it happened.

But we don't judge a person's worth through the rest of life on the basis of the difficulty or the drama of his entrance into this world—and neither should we determine a person's spiri-tual worth on the basis of the peculiar circumstances of his conversion. The main issue in human life is that a person is alive, whatever the circumstances of birth, and the main issue in spiritual life is that a person is demonstrably Christian, whether the entry to faith came by vision, tears, and heavenly voices, or by a long, apparently simple, rather undramatic process.

We don't know about James's conversion. We can probably assume that it was not dramatic enough to deserve a record in the New Testament story. But we *do* know that he was called by Christ, and that he became a disciple. And obviously his conversion and call, lacking in sensation though they may have been, were just as valid as the experiences of Simon Peter and Saul of Tarsus.

Nor do we know anything about James's work. We have no listing of his achievements, no accounting of the souls he won to God. But this doesn't mean that he was inactive or that he was ineffective. To the contrary, we have every reason to assume that James the Less was as busy as any other of the dis-ciples, preaching, teaching, healing the sick, casting out demons, blessing others with the riches of Christ that had blessed him. We can be sure that if James had avoided work or if he had not measured up to the high standards of discipleship, the New Testament would have singled him out for reprimand. Come to think of it, while there is no record of his achievements, in the style of Andrew or Peter, neither is there any record of his being reproved, as were Peter, John, the other James, and Thomas.

Several things should probably be said about the work of James the Less. For one, he must have been the kind of person whose work simply never attracts attention. Some folk do their work with such a flair and a flourish that you can almost hear the trumpets blow as they make their rounds. In our publicity-conscious times, you can reasonably guess that the person blowing the trumpet is either the one whose name is being mentioned, or someone hired by him or her.

But others go about their work so quietly that we don't always realize they're at work, until we're surprised to see the task completed. I think James may have been that kind of person. Jesus demanded the utmost from his disciples; we can conclude that James fulfilled those high demands, but that he did so in such a manner that the Gospels find no reason to report on his work. And perhaps his work happened, by chance, to be in obscure occasions, or in matters superficially routine.

Another word should also be said. God judges us, not on the basis of how much we accomplish, but on the basis of how much we do in light of what we are capable of doing. Heaven doesn't have a time-study program that calculates that every person should be able to produce a certain number of units of spirituality. God remembers our frame, that we are dust—and perhaps also the specific quality of our particular dust. Some persons of apparently notable achievements may well be censured in heaven for not having done more, in light of their capacities, while others who have gone through life with little fanfare may by eternity's measure have done extraordinarily well with modest equipment and opportunity.

We don't know what James did. But whatever it was, apparently our Lord considered it adequate and right for James. When an ordinary person (whatever that may mean!) does ordinary tasks faithfully, he or she is as worthy of praise as the presumably heroic person who easily performs acts of heroism. I'm grateful that God is a knowing judge, observing us individually and personally on the basis of the equipment with which we work, and the kind of field in which we labor. Only an observer of such capacity can estimate our work fairly.

When we call this disciple James the Less, the name itself seems an irony. Among the twelve apostles there were two named James. People didn't have family names as such in those days, so something extra was needed in order to identify persons with the same surname. Often it was a person's town; thus, "Jesus of Nazareth." More often it might be the reference to the father's name, as with John "son of Zebedee."

So one James in the apostolic band was known as "James, the son of Zebedee," while sometimes the James of whom we now speak was known as "James, son of Alphaeus." But apparently people also knew him by the perhaps not-too-complimentary title "James the Less."

This term could have meant several things. Perhaps "less" means "younger," as it is translated in the New Revised Standard Version, which suggests that of the two men named James in the apostolic company, he was the younger. Or perhaps it was a reference to his height, if he were particularly short. Or perhaps (and this may be the most likely of all) this was simply an expression of the standing of the two men with the same surname: There was James, the brother of John, who was a leader in the body of the disciples, and part of the inner circle of three; and then there was this James. So when someone mentioned "James," people might ask, "Do you mean the big James, the important one, or the other one?" And it may be that the name began to stick with this one: James the *Less*.

Well, it isn't the designation you would choose, is it? No matter how you look at it, it comes out the same way; slice it as you will, it's still thin. In a culture where age was revered, he was James the younger, if that was the pattern of judgment. If a matter of physical appearance, I think it's never too pleasant to be identified in comparison, whether they name you Shorty, Fatso, Skinny, or Big Stoop. And to be identified simply as the less important person in a tandem—well, who wants to be reminded daily that he or she is inferior? But that's what they called him: "James the Less."

In truth, we don't know much about the kind of person James was, but I'm confident he had a great spirit. The pattern of his life didn't fall in impressive, important places. And with that the case, what adjustments of soul did James have to make? I'm sure that at times, especially in his earlier manhood, James dreamed (as so many of us do) that someday he would be admired, important, looked-up-to. In their place, such dreams aren't wrong. Often they're the fuel of achievement.

But if James had such dreams, we have to conclude that they never worked out. He was called to follow Jesus, but his call must have been relatively matter-of-fact and routine, unmarked by the uniqueness that characterized some of the others. He became one of the privileged Twelve, but never more than a name on the list. Apparently he did the work to which he was called, but never with a flourish. And while the crowds were fascinated by the power of Peter and amused by the cynical humor of Thomas and enchanted by the attractiveness of John the beloved, they could hardly have noticed that James the Less was on the team.

Yet he did his work, and we have every reason to believe that he did it well. While we're told nothing of his accomplishing anything noteworthy, neither is there any evidence of his ever being unfaithful to his Lord. Rather, we have to assume that his whole record was one of quiet, unheralded loyalty.

Legend says that James the Less was asked to renounce Christ. Instead, he cried in a loud voice that Jesus was the Son of God. When he did so, he was thrown to the ground from the battlements of the Temple. James survived the fall and began to pray for those who were abusing him. They, in turn, began to stone him. At last a fuller standing nearby struck out James's life with a blow on the head. Then his persecutors, in a torrent of brutality, sawed his body to pieces before he was buried. Because of the nature of his death and dismemberment, a saw and sometimes a fuller's club are used as the emblems of this apostle.

I'm glad we know as much as we do about the more dramatic lives of Simon Peter, John, and Matthew. But I think I'm as glad, and perhaps even more so, that we know so little about James the Less. There's something encouraging in the fact that our Lord had room in the sacred company of the Twelve for a man of apparently modest gifts and obscure achievements. Perhaps I hold him in special affection because during my nearly forty years as a pastor, I came to appreciate the sterling quality of such persons.

So he's only a name in the list, unpretentious in call and in accomplishments, but with his own place of dignity as an apostle of Jesus Christ. James, son of Alphaeus—commonly known as James the Less. He is the apostle of those who are faithful but easily forgotten or overlooked. In the kingdom of heaven, his may be the largest contingent of all.

CHAPTER 6
SIMON, THE ZEALOT

READ LUKE 6:12-25.

When you and I think of the apostles, we usually get caught in a "stained-glass syndrome." We see the apostles as finished products: devout, unswerving, and possessing great singleness of purpose. We forget that when Jesus called them, they were not picture saints, but human beings. *Very* human. Of course, God makes all saints from human stuff, but we're likely to forget that this is the case, especially when the persons involved lived in a different and far-off time.

So we may not easily realize that the disciples probably followed Jesus with mixed motives. We're impressed by the miracle of their conversions, as we should be, and with the quality of their continuing dedication. In our marveling, however, we lose sight of the complexity of our human emotions and motivations. Whenever we humans make a decision or a choice, a multitude of elements help to shape it. I dare to say that everything that has ever happened to us, everything that has ever been said to us, and everything we have ever learned, consciously or unconsciously, influences our decisions at any given moment.

If this is so in general, I'm certain it's especially true in that most significant of all decisions, religious conversion. The Spirit of God doesn't operate in a vacuum; it deals with the stuff of our daily lives. God meets us where we are and speaks to us in the circumstances of our unique, individual lives.

Sometimes, in fact, it seems that the Holy Spirit finds voice in the very uniqueness of our particular circumstances and personality. And how could it be otherwise, because no one respects our human personality more than the God who has endowed us with the stuff of personhood.

So when a person comes to Christ, it isn't surprising that he or she comes with mixed motives. The great emotion of the moment may be love or devotion, hope or despair. But other emotions will also be at work, many of them so far below the surface that we can't easily isolate or identify them.

Take the apostle named Simon the Zealot. What was in his mind when he chose to follow Jesus Christ? We're not told, but on the basis of his name, it's easy to speculate reasonably. In the listing of the apostles, Simon is always identified as "the Zealot" or as "the Cananaean." The second term, *Cananaean*, is not a geographical term, as we might ordinarily think, telling us where Simon was born; it simply means "Zealot" in another language.

The New Revised Standard Version capitalizes both Cananaean and Zealot, to indicate that the words are identifying titles. We use the word *zealot* today to describe a person who is passionate for a cause or a movement. But in the first century, it was the name of a particular movement, so it is rightly capitalized—just as today we capitalize Democrat or Republican when we refer to a political party.

The first century Zealots were a fierce lot. They were the last of the great Jewish political parties to emerge, and they were the most fervent patriots of all. Born in Galilee near the beginning of the first century, they came into existence in reaction to a Roman program of taxation. The Galileans were a passionate people, apparently always ready for any exciting new idea. Thus when a certain Galilean named Judas (not the apostle Judas) called for revolt against the Romans, before long he had gathered around him a vigorous band of his fellow Galileans.

Their first attempt at revolt was rather easily broken, but before long Judas was at it again, this time in opposition to the census and taxation that came under Cyrenius. But this time the issue was not simply taxation, but religion. Judas reasoned that tribute should be paid only to God, and when a Gentile government called for taxes, it was tantamount to asking the Jews to violate their faith. This time the Romans not only crushed the revolt, they killed Judas. It was his death that brought the Zealots into existence.

They became an underground movement. They took a slogan that was like a blood bond: "No king but the Lord; no tax but the temple; no friend but a Zealot." They were a force to be reckoned with all through Jesus' lifetime and for a generation after his crucifixion. But in their efforts to deliver the Jews from Rome, ·' ·y succeeded only in bringing about the destruction of Jerus .em.

But keep this in mind. The Zealots were not simply Jewish patriots; they were intensely religious. This can be an explosive combination. The union of fervent patriotism and religious commitment is an almost irresistible force. The Zealots envisioned Israel as a nation ruled by God and by God alone, and they were fiercely devoted to liberty. The Jewish historian Josephus said that they did not mind dying any kind of death, would not be moved by the torture of kindred or friends, and that no fear could make them call any man lord (*Antiquities*, 18, 1, 6, quoted in William Barclay, *The Master's Men*, Abingdon Press, 1959; page 96).

When one is so thoroughly committed to a cause, the enemy soon is seen as anyone who is not equally committed. Zealots came to hate many of their own countrymen as bitterly as they hated the Romans. Many Jews had come to feel they had no choice but to live with the Romans and to endure Roman occupation; after all, Rome's power was overwhelming. The Zealots wouldn't countenance such reasoning. In their fanaticism, some Zealots became Assassins, known for their small, curved sword, the *sica*, which they carried hidden in their robes. Today such a movement would be described as terrorists. They killed not only Romans, but also Jews who seemed to them to hold a too conciliatory position.

Probably the best way to help us get the flavor of the Zealots is to remind ourselves of how the last of them died. When Jerusalem fell, some forty years after the crucifixion of our Lord, the last of the strongholds where resistance was maintained was a rugged mountain fortress called Masada. If you visit Israel today, this is one of the places you will almost surely be taken. When the Zealot who led the Masada group (a descendant of the earlier Judas, by the way) saw that there was no hope, he made a passionate speech urging the men to slaughter their own wives and children first, then take their own lives. But by no means were they to allow the Romans to capture them. According to Josephus, this is just what they did: "They tenderly embraced their wives, kissed their children, and then began the bloody work. Nine hundred and sixty perished; only two women and five children escaped by hiding in a cave" (*The Wars of the Jews*, 7, 8, 9, quoted in Barclay, *The Master's Men*; page 97).

These were the Zealots, and this is the party to which Simon belonged. Now why would a person with such fanatical and unrestrained nationalist views become a disciple of Jesus? If your only picture of Jesus is that conveyed in the words "Gentle Jesus, meek and mild," you'll never understand how Simon could have followed him. Obviously there was more to Jesus than his gentle side. His physical presence must have carried dynamic strength. He had the gentleness to attract little children to himself and to heal the sick, but he also had the sinewy vigor to draw rugged men to his cause. Most of the disciples were Galileans, the most intensely patriotic and volatile of the Jews. Most of them had grown up in the very area where the Zealot movement was strongest and where the stories of Zealot heroism were household legends. Why would such persons rally around Jesus, including especially Simon, a sworn member of the Zealot party?

To find the answer, we have to look at the New Testament with first-century Jewish eyes, rather than twenty-first-century Western eyes. Think for a moment how often Jesus spoke about "the kingdom of God" or "the kingdom of heaven." You and I are disposed to see those terms in a theological way, but to a person like Simon, who merged politics and theology into a single whole, and who was seeking to establish a government where God was king, such a term would almost surely be seen as the language of revolution.

Think, too, of some of the things Jesus said—for example, Luke's version of the Sermon on the Mount (Luke 6:17-49). His Gospel gives us this message just after the choosing of the Twelve, as if this were their ordination sermon. Perhaps in a sense, it was. At any rate, many of the sayings that are part of that sermon must have been said many times in the course of Jesus' teaching. As you read these words (aloud or otherwise), see if you can place yourself in the shoes of Simon, a fervent Jewish revolutionary. Imagine Simon coming one day to a place where Jesus was speaking—Simon the Zealot, fevered with desire to overthrow Rome and to establish a righteous government—and his hearing Jesus speak these words:

> "Blessed are you who are poor,
>   for yours is the kingdom of God.
> "Blessed are you who are hungry now,
>   for you will be filled.
>
> . . . .
>
> "But woe to you who are rich,
>   for you have received your consolation.
> "Woe to you who are full now,
>   for you will be hungry." (Luke 6:20-21, 24-25).

I think if I had been Simon and had heard Jesus say, "Woe to the rich, woe to the full; blessed are the poor, blessed are the hungry," something in me would have said, "This is the leader of my dreams! A greater one than our martyred Judas is here! Surely this is the one who will restore the kingdom to Israel."

And if Simon felt that way, he wasn't alone among the disciples. Apparently a number of them saw Jesus as the deliverer of Israel and thought that he would fulfill the role by leading a successful revolt against Rome. Even after Jesus' resurrection, when he was commanding the disciples to tarry in Jerusalem to seek the Holy Spirit, some of them asked, "Lord, is this the time when you will restore the kingdom to Israel?" (Acts 1:6).

So it is not surprising if Simon the Zealot, a man whose piosity expressed itself in political action, was drawn to Jesus. I am not by any means suggesting that Simon wasn't truly converted; quite the contrary. Nor am I suggesting that Simon's view of Jesus was primarily political. I am only saying that Simon the Zealot, the man of fierce patriotism, found himself at home with Jesus, and that as he began to follow him, Simon may well have envisioned a great new movement under the direction of this Jesus of Nazareth.

But what an adjustment Simon must have made! When he became part of the little group of the Twelve, he found himself a partner with Matthew, who had formerly been a tax collector. I can't imagine a more impossible relationship. If there were anyone for whom Simon would feel instinctive and vehement loathing, it would be a Jew who had turned traitor to his people by becoming a tax collector for Rome. Matthew was the very kind of person Zealots like Simon would make victim to their *sica*. Now, instead, he found that he must eat, sleep, talk, pray, and form strong ties of community with such a one. To a Zealot, the only person lower than a Roman had to be a Jew who would collaborate with the Romans; and that's what Simon found in the fellowship of the apostles—a former tax collector. "Put your arm around him, Simon; call him *Brother.*"

In this we have both the glory and the discomfort of the Christian church. Most of us tend naturally to seek out our own kind of people. We are usually more comfortable with those who are like us. Sometimes it's a matter of ethnic bonds, sometimes economic, sometimes cultural, intellectual, social, or political. People join a Ukrainian Society because they want to be with other Ukrainians, or a golf club because they enjoy the company of other golfers; or they find their friends in a university community because they enjoy a certain style of conversation and cultural interchange.

Consider, then, the unlikely nature of a Christian church. In the first such community there was a man named Zealot, and a man formerly a Roman collaborationist; now, they belonged to one another. I think of the last congregation of which I was the pastor. I suppose most people would have assumed that it was very homogeneous. Nevertheless, we had in it some who had never finished high school, and others with earned doctorates; we had Republicans, Democrats, and Mugwumps. I knew that some would leave an estate measured in the millions of dollars, while others hoped simply to be buried with dignity. Some of my people thought there was nothing more enjoyable than to go in evening dress to hear the Metropolitan opera, while others cherished shirt sleeves at the baseball stadium. Yet on Sunday mornings we came together in one place, to sing the same hymns, to unite in prayer, and to involve ourselves in the same sermon.

The church is often criticized for not doing a better job with race relations, and as someone who has been committed to that cause since I was a boy in the eighth grade, I am pained that we haven't done better. But I also marvel that we've done as well as we have. People who like cute slogans sometimes say that eleven o'clock Sunday morning is the most segregated hour of the week. In truth, it is the hour of the week when the largest number of people integrate voluntarily. Most other integration comes by law or by economic necessity. Much as I wish that more churches were more effectively integrated, I know of no other voluntary organization—service club, fraternity / sorority, or social club—that brings more racial and ethnic variety.

We do indeed tend to associate with those whose interests and topics of conversation are compatible with our own; yet the church brings together in any single congregation a remarkable variety of different and often competing and antagonistic interests. Jesus had this in his little group of Twelve, with Matthew and Simon, and a church is less than Jesus meant it to be if it cannot bring together different kinds and classes of persons. Jesus Christ is Lord, and that loyalty overarches our ethnic, economic, social, cultural, and intellectual differences.

The Bible tells us nothing of Simon the Zealot after the Resurrection, except that he stayed with the band of disciples. The dream of an earthly kingdom was gone, but the reality of Jesus Christ, Lord and Master, remained. Some tradition says that Simon preached in the British Isles. Most agree that he took the gospel to Persia and was probably martyred there—perhaps with battle-ax and saw. But this we know for sure: Simon the Zealot, the political activist who was attracted to Jesus with mixed motives (as are all of us, in our conversions to him), stayed with Jesus because Jesus became his Lord, his *ultimate* loyalty.

And so, please, may it be with all of us. This is, indeed, the Kingdom that he came to bring, a Kingdom that Simon joined—as all of us do—with limited understanding, and for which he died with magnificent fullness.

CHAPTER 7
NATHANAEL, THE FORTHRIGHT

READ JOHN 1:43-51.

Little children charm us by their directness. We quote what they say because their incidental remarks go straight through the tedium, detail, and subterfuge of life. They ask big questions with unpracticed candor. A small boy may interrupt his *varooming* sounds as he plays with his cars to ask, without prelude, "Why do people die?" or "What's God like?" Children charm us because they're forthright, and we adults observe this quality, delight in it, then struggle to be just the opposite, as we train ourselves to be guarded, cautious, and tentative.

The apostle Nathanael was the childlike one. When Jesus first met him, he singled out this quality of forthrightness for special notice and praise.

Nathanael, like so many of the apostles, was probably a fisherman by trade. He is also known as Bartholomew. He came from the city of Cana in Galilee, the city where Jesus worked his first miracle. As a matter of fact, there's a tradition that when Jesus worked his miracle at the Cana wedding, the bridegroom was Nathanael. There's no substantial proof for this theory, only the kind of speculation that so much appeals to us. But it's an old legend, nevertheless.

As I mentioned earlier, we call this man both Nathanael and Bartholomew. I should say a word about the confusion in names. The name of Nathanael is not mentioned among the disciples in the first three Gospels; there, a man named

Bartholomew is always listed. By contrast, the fourth Gospel never mentions a Bartholomew, but it makes a good bit of Nathanael. Are the two men one and the same?

Most likely. Perhaps the best evidence is this: In the first three Gospels, the names of Philip and Bartholomew are always associated, while in the fourth Gospel the name of Philip is tied with Nathanael. Also, *Bartholomew* is not a first name, it is an identifying second name—the kind that in ancient times singled out a man from others of the same name by using the name of his father. *Bar* means "son of"; thus, *Bartholomew* means literally "son of Tolmai." On the weight of these details and other general evidence, we judge that Bartholomew was the second name of the apostle named Nathanael.

As far as the biblical record is concerned, the story of Nathanael is the story of his call to follow Christ. The Bible tells us virtually nothing more about him, but it gives more detail to his call than to that of any other disciple. This may be at least partly because the story of Nathanael's call provides us with such a fascinating key to his total character.

Nathanael's conversion and call could have been expected, because Nathanael was seeking. I believe that every person looks for a faith at some time during his or her life; indeed, probably numbers of times. Some seem more faith-driven than others, but this perception may only mean that we don't know all that goes on in any given person's soul. Some are driven to seek God by sickness, defeat, bereavement, or an unnamed sense of emptiness and longing. But some seem to seek without such external pressures; they hunger for God, not because they are in trouble, but because they seem to have some innate longing.

I don't think anyone can satisfactorily say why this is so. It's not simply heredity or environment, because within any given family you will sometimes see one sibling with such a passionate longing, while another is blasé about things of the Spirit. The current emphasis on the genetic code will probably persuade some that spiritual longing is nothing other than one of the elements in that code. I doubt it. I think our spiritual inclination is probably more complex than can be explained in any summary fashion. The times themselves play a part, as do our associations, both casual and sustained. Then, there's the Spirit of God: Jesus said that the wind of the Spirit "blows where it chooses, and you hear the sound of it, but you do not know where it comes from or where it goes" (John 3:8). Rather than occupying ourselves with asking why some are more Spirit-driven than others, I expect that we should make certain that we respond to the urgings that come our way— and that we should be instrumental in opening more possibilities of this kind to others.

But in Nathanael's case, there's a strange turn. He is the only disciple who seemed to hesitate in responding to God's call. Mind you, every New Testament record of an apostolic conversion is too brief, from our point of view, because the Bible puts its material so succinctly. Thus even Nathanael's story has less detail than we would like. Nevertheless, the contrast is clear: Where the other conversion stories show Jesus calling someone and that person rising up without delay, Nathanael engages in a dialogue of sorts, first with Philip, then with Jesus.

It was Philip who brought Nathanael to Jesus. Philip had met the Master, and immediately he reported his experience to his friend Nathanael. Philip's report was enthusiastic: "We've found him!" I think we can rightly deduce, from Philip's approach to Nathanael, that the two of them had been studying and searching for some time, and that they were looking for the coming of either the Messiah himself or the messenger who would prepare the way for the Messiah.

So Philip reported, "We have found him about whom

Moses in the law and also the prophets wrote, Jesus son of Joseph from Nazareth" (John 1:45). I see four or five elements in Philip's sentence that might have evoked a response from Nathanael, but Nathanael fastened his attention on just one, the reference to the city of Nazareth. "Can anything good come out of Nazareth?" he asked (John 1:46).

What was in Nathanael's mind, to elicit such a sharply negative reaction? It may have had to do with Nathanael's reasoning as a student of the Scriptures. He had no doubt learned that Nazareth was mentioned by none of the prophets. In fact, Nazareth had done nothing to win a place in Jewish history or affection. It had produced no poet, no king, no notable prophet. Nazareth didn't seem to rate on heaven's timetable, past or present. Nathanael may well have reasoned that God was hardly likely to bring the Messiah from a city unmentioned in prophecy and unheralded for any achievement.

But it's quite possible there was also a petty human element. As I mentioned earlier, Nathanael came from Cana, and Cana and Nazareth were neighboring villages. If there had been high-school basketball and football teams in those days, these two towns would have been natural rivals. When familiarity and rivalry are joined, they're almost certain to breed contempt. Jesus was later to say that a prophet is without honor in his own country; Nathanael's remark may partake of this same mood. Most of us are a little like Nathanael: We can't really imagine that a person from the next town or the next street could be majestically important. Not really!

But Philip had the perfect answer for his friend. When Nathanael asked his rather condescending question, Philip replied, "Come and see." The two men had obviously studied together. Philip therefore confronted Nathanael with a scholar's challenge: *Come and see.* "Find out for yourself; take a look at the evidence." How can a thinking person write off a possibility if he or she hasn't looked? So Nathanael went to see Jesus and was immediately taken off guard. While he was still approaching our Lord, Jesus seemed to look deep into his soul. "Here is truly an Israelite in whom there is no deceit!" (John 1:47). The late William Barclay suggests that any devout Israelite would recognize such a statement as a particular compliment. The Jewish Scriptures repeatedly praised the person who was without guile or deceit. Think, for instance, of Psalm 32:2: "Happy are those . . . in whose spirit there is no deceit."

With one short sentence, Jesus identified the quality that most characterized Nathanael. He was a forthright human being—guileless, transparent, perhaps even naïve. There were no hidden agendas in his style, nothing said to mislead, nothing done simply for effect. When Philip first told Nathanael about Jesus, Nathanael spoke his doubts without hesitation or apology, even to the point of abruptness. It was this very quality of openness that Jesus praised.

Most of us don't grow very old before we learn to avoid such directness. We learn, by both precept and example, to hide many of our deepest feelings, lest by revealing them we offend someone or make ourselves vulnerable. I repeat, this is a trained response. Children aren't this way until they catch on to the adult style. They express their likes and dislikes with what is at times distressing candor, not hesitating to throw their arms around someone they love or to retreat from someone they fear. Mind you, this childlike quality needs some tempering and modifying, but not to the degree that most of us bring to pass. The purpose of words, gestures, and facial expressions is to communicate, but society trains us to use these instruments to conceal and even to deceive. How ironic!

When Jesus greeted Nathanael by praising his guilelessness, Nathanael quickly countered, "Where did you get to know me?" Jesus had complimented him, but in a manner that plumbed his personality. Jesus replied, "I saw you under the fig tree before Philip called you." Something about this matter-of-fact, yet rather enigmatic statement seemed to awe Nathanael, so that he cried, "Rabbi, you are the Son of God! You are the King of Israel!" (John 1:48-49).

We can do some speculating between the lines, using some logic with our speculation. William Barclay explains that in the cultural pattern of that first-century world, the houses of poorer people usually had only one room, but they would often have a fig tree at the door of their cottage. The tree would grow to a height of about fifteen feet, and its branches would get a spread of as much as twenty-five feet. This fig tree just outside the cottage was often seen as a kind of private room. When people wanted a quiet place to meditate and pray, they went under their fig tree (see William Barclay, *The Master's Men*, Abingdon Press, 1959; page 111). Rabbis recognized this practice and described a seat under a fig tree as the right place for study of the Torah (*The Interpreter's Bible*, vol. 8, Abingdon Press, 1952; page 489).

So when Jesus said, "I saw you under the fig tree," the inference was, "I know you're a devout man, one who searches the law of God." It's as if a teacher in our day were to say to a student, "I've noticed how much time you spend in the library," or if a priest were to say to a parishioner, "I see you in Mass nearly every morning."

Whatever the setting, and however much the Gospel writer may have abbreviated the story, it's clear that Nathanael was deeply moved. After all, so many of life's encounters can't be adequately communicated simply by quoting the conversation; as we sometimes say when reporting an incident to a friend, "You'd have to have been there to understand it." Nathanael had been studying and longing, perhaps for years. Now he saw in Jesus the end to his search and the fulfillment of his dreams. So, forthright man that he was, he made the ultimate confession: "You are the Son of God!"

Jesus' reply to Nathanael seems almost playful. He said, in effect, "Are you so easily convinced? You'll see a great deal more in time to come." But Nathanael was true to his guileless, open temperament; as surely as he at first discredited Jesus for coming from Nazareth, now he accepted him without reservation, and in ultimate language.

The Bible doesn't tell us anything about Nathanael as a preacher or as a worker. One wonders what kind of preacher such a forthright soul would be! Probably some found him naïve, while others were turned off by his candor. And what kind of counselor might he have been? He certainly wouldn't have fit in the nondirective camp! And how did he take his place with the other apostles? They were probably all a bit more forthright than we are in our time and place, yet Nathanael alone is identified for his guileless nature. How did he and Judas relate, especially when Judas began to edge toward betrayal? And did James and John feel uneasy around this open, honest man when they were jockeying for places of leadership at Jesus' right hand? When we have a hidden agenda, guileless people are likely to make us uncomfortable. I wonder if the other disciples depended on Nathanael to keep them honest?

But on the other hand, Nathanael shouldn't be held up as an untarnished model. To be without deceit doesn't mean simply to be frank. Some people are frank precisely because they are full of guile; that's where we get the term "brutally frank." The New Testament commands us to speak the truth in love (Ephesians 4:15). It's often difficult enough to speak the truth, but it's far more difficult to speak it *in love*. Some find evil pleasure in telling (or preaching) the truth because of the pain it brings to others. I don't think this was Nathanael's quality. There was no deceit in him, no using candor for personal advantage. Though a forthright man, he was not an unkind one.

The Bible mentions Nathanael only one other time, but it

is a significant reference. It happens during the first days after Jesus' crucifixion and resurrection, when the disciples seemed to be groping their way toward an understanding of their new role. Nathanael is listed among the group who went fishing with Simon Peter, and who then had a particularly moving encounter with the risen Christ (John 21:2). But he is mentioned only as one of the group, with no further identification.

Tradition and legend credit Nathanael with missionary journeys to several parts of the world. One especially dramatic story says that he and Philip continued to work together and were at last apprehended in Hierapolis of Phrygia. They were nailed opposite each other, so each could see the other's suffering. But Philip prayed for Nathanael's release, and, according to this tradition, his prayer was answered.

After that, the report continues, Nathanael took the gospel to parts of India, then returned to preach in Armenia. There the king of Albanopolis ordered a brutal flaying of Nathanael, to his death and martyrdom. Thus the flaying knife is often the symbol that represents Nathanael in stained-glass windows and other forms of remembrance.

For me, however, Nathanel will always be the man without deceit, a forthright human being, charming in his childike directness. I see him outside a modest cottage, reading the Scriptures under a spreading fig tree. I hear him scoffing the prospect of God's Messiah coming from the despised neighboring town of Nazareth. Then I see him awestruck before Jesus, making the grand confession, "You are the Son of God!"

We can never know for sure whether Nathanael's apostleship took him, as tradition and legend report, to Phrygia, India, and Armenia, or to places of which we have no record. But faith—and perhaps sentiment—tell me that his openness and his unspoiled enthusiasm brought the radiance of faith to anyone whose path crossed his. I'd like to have been among them, to have met Nathanael, the forthright.

CHAPTER 8
*M*ATTHEW, THE SUCCESSFUL MAN

READ MATTHEW 9:9-11.

Many years ago, I was associated with a Hollywood musician at the time of his conversion and during the early development of his Christian life. I reported the good news to a friend who was also in the entertainment business. He dismissed the news cynically. "I'm not surprised to hear he's been converted. Hey, look, he's no longer at the top."

My friend was reflecting a common theory, that people turn to God only in the midst of failure or deep trouble. There's more than a little substance to this theory, of course. We are often driven to God by the harsh winds of failure; and by contrast, people who are courting success often find their achievements so all-involving and so consuming that the need for God seems hardly to enter their minds.

But now and again, persons turn to God right in the midst of a winning streak. Success, you know, is a mysterious creature. Nothing on earth seems to matter so much when you don't have it and when you're pursuing it. But often nothing matters less once it is achieved. Success is a perfume whose aroma tantalizes from a distance, but often proves dull—yes, even gross—at close range.

We have no evidence that any of the apostles were failures when Christ came into their lives. Since they were all relatively young men, I think we can assume that defeat hadn't yet forcibly possessed them. Not that young people don't know the meaning of defeat; far from it. But when we are young, we have remarkable resiliency. Tuesday's defeat is lost in Wednesday's laughter. Yet while the disciples were still too young to have been taken captive by defeat, they were also too young to have gained any measure of success. They were doing well, but not to a degree that their winnings were likely to consume them.

Except for Matthew. He was probably just a little older than the others, and he qualified as a success, as we humans often measure success. But in the midst of his success, with so much going his way and with the promise of still better tomorrows, Matthew rose up and left it all to follow Jesus Christ.

Let me pause a moment to say that success is many things to many people. If beauty is in the eye of the beholder, success is in the vision of the seeker. For some, success means bottom-line wealth; for others, it means being "All-Pro." The novel-ist wants to write a best seller, but the scholar hopes to publish an esoteric monograph that (with good fortune) no more than two or three hundred will ever read. Success must have as many definitions as the number of persons pursuing it.

Matthew was a success, at least by some generally popular standards. He was no doubt very well-to-do, and he had every possibility of becoming still richer. There was a lot of money to be made in his profession, and it was a field reasonably secure from depression or inflation. And he probably had a good number of friends within his profession.

But I doubt that he had any friends outside it, because Matthew's work was despised by the world at large. Matthew was a tax collector.

Now, I've known a few tax collectors and have found them to be a generally pleasant lot—sometimes a little neurotic about details, but not unkind. I remember, in fact, a state offi-cial, checking out something by telephone, who suddenly interrupted my explanation to say, with mid-South warmth,

"You have the nicest voice!" (More important, she eventually decided that my records were correct.)

But you and I have not had to deal with tax collectors in the first-century world. When Cicero, the Roman statesman from the century before Matthew's time, listed trades unbecoming to a gentleman, he called tax collectors and usurers (lenders of money at high interest) the most reprehensible. Cicero's opinion would probably have been popularly endorsed, because tax collectors were the living symbol of graft and corruption. For a time, the Roman government farmed out its tax areas to the highest bidder, in what we would today call franchises. A person agreed to pay the government a stated sum for the tax area, and anything he collected beyond that sum was his own. It's easy to see the kind of graft such a system encouraged. In some instances, corporate bodies bought large sections of provinces to become the taxing agency of the area.

In Jesus' day, the Romans used three main taxes: a ground tax of one-tenth of grain and one-fifth of fruit, a poll tax that every adult had to pay, and an income tax of one percent. (Some moderns might observe that those were, indeed, the good old days!) But there were numbers of other taxes, including a duty on everything imported and exported; sales tax on things bought and sold; and taxes to travel on main roads, cross bridges, or enter marketplaces, towns, and harbors. Traveling on certain roads, you might have to pay a tax to use the road, a tax on your cart, a tax on its wheels, a tax on its axle, and a tax on the animal pulling the cart! That, it seems to me, would be enough to make a person stay home. And it should be evidence enough that, although our generation has become quite sophisticated in developing methods of taxation, the art (if I may call it that) has a long history.

But not only were the tax collectors notoriously dishonest, and the taxes offensive, as far as the Jews were concerned, tax collectors were traitors. I mentioned this in the chapter on Simon the Zealot, so I won't enlarge upon it here except to say that the first-century Jews felt that anyone from their nation who would aid the Romans by becoming a tax collector was the lowest of creatures. Such a person was not only barred from being either a witness or a judge, he was even barred from worship.

So here we have Matthew, our subject of the moment, and our potential hero. He was a Jew who had turned traitor to his own people, to his heritage, and to his God, in order to become a success. And he had made it! He was a Roman tax agent, with a good income and the promise of a secure future. Now we find him one morning, at his custom desk, set for another prosperous day. Already the money had begun to pile up. If Matthew was as good a businessman as I think he was, he worked each day with a personal goal, that by a certain hour of the day, he would have met the cost of his franchise for this day, as carefully measured out through the year. Matthew was no doubt impartial; if he cheated a taxpayer here, and the government there, he would meet his quota by early afternoon, and the rest of the day's proceeds, as they say, would be "gravy."

Matthew's customs office was probably by the seashore, near the border, so the whole world seemed to pass by his desk. There were businessmen from Rome, a scholar fresh from the schools of Athens, Arab sheiks with the mystery of the desert still upon them, a group of travelers from Syria.

Then, in the midst of the crowd, stood a solitary figure. He was surrounded by people, yet he stood out as if he were inescapably singular.

The New Testament, in the book bearing Matthew's name, says it this way: "As Jesus was walking along, he saw a man called Matthew sitting at the tax booth" (Matthew 9:9). What did Jesus see? A Jew who had turned traitor to his own people? A man so hungry for success that he was buying it with various-sized portions of his honor? Perhaps a cheating, conniving, grasping Scrooge? What did Jesus see when he looked at the man called Matthew?

I tell you, he saw a saint in the making; a man who could be an apostle, who would love to tell the Story; a man, indeed, who would heal the sick and spread the faith, a man who could play a part in writing a Gospel. Jesus called Simon and Andrew from their fishing boats to become fishers of men; did he anticipate making Matthew a dealer in the eternal coin of the Kingdom?

Even for those who believe in miracles, Jesus had chosen an unlikely place to find a potential saint. In a job that made a person ineligible for Jewish worship, a position that implied traitorism, and a business that counted for sharp dealing and even dishonesty for its profit, what were the odds of finding Saint Matthew? But you see, the Spirit of God always hovers over our souls in unlikely places. It seems that God saw the potential of Augustine when he was consumed with lust and the possibilities of a Charles Colson when he was immersed in the shame of Watergate. So what about the people who seem to me to be of little or no worth? What, indeed, about *me?*

Then came the moment of truth. The New Testament tells the story so succinctly (as is its pattern) that it seems terribly simple, even to the point of abbreviation: "And [Jesus] said to him, 'Follow me.' And he got up and followed him" (Matthew 9:9). One can't help asking what story is behind those words. Surely Matthew had heard Jesus teach and preach prior to this encounter. Was there also some prior conversation? And what of Matthew's heritage; had he grown up in a godly Jewish home, from which he had rebelled but had never been able fully to escape?

A world of drama must lie behind those words that appear in Matthew 9:9. Two men are locked in the eternal issue of the soul. One is set in affluence and monetary security; the other is rich in faith and mission. The Master loves this businessman, and wants him. For a moment it seems there is no person in the bustling marketplace but these two, and for a moment all the voices of sale and barter, the cries of pack animals, the noises of the street are silent, so that the man at the customs desk hears only two words. The universe has grown still so a questionable tax collector can hear the voice of God: *Follow me*.

> Wait for a moment, Matthew. Look at your customs table, your business, this familiar setting. Remember how hard you have worked to get this. Success isn't easy to come by, man; better hold tight to it.
> And think, too, what you'll have to give up, Matthew: your job, because the business you're in won't fit with this Man; your security; your future.

So Matthew looked at his business, his security, the familiar surroundings (familiarity, even in places that aren't necessarily attractive, is so compelling), his success. And he looked at Jesus of Nazareth, the Christ—"and he got up and followed him."

That's how Matthew became a disciple. And do you know what he did next? He threw a party, to celebrate his newfound faith. We have parties because we're a year older, or because someone has graduated from somewhere, or perhaps simply to bring together some of our friends, or perhaps only to fulfill a social obligation. Matthew had one because he had found God and had just lost his job. And do you know who he invited to the party? Jesus, of course, was the guest of honor. The rest of the party guests were Matthew's tax collector friends and a few other disreputable folk—the only friends Matthew could keep in his former occupation.

I find myself with a question. Matthew's first social occasion after his conversion was one that centered on Jesus. How many of mine—of ours—are built around our religious life or are intended to bring praise to Christ? Or is it possible that our social life is still open to conversion?

Dr. Alexander Whyte, a great preacher of the late nineteenth and early twentieth centuries, used to say that the only thing Matthew took with him when he rose up to follow Jesus was his pen and ink. According to Irenaeus, Matthew preached the gospel to the Hebrews; at any rate, the New Testament book that bears his name is the one especially tailored to the Jewish mind, with its emphasis on genealogy, numbers, and Old Testament prophecies. Some scholars feel that the Gospel that bears his name couldn't have come directly from him, but that rather it is a summary of his memories and teachings as recorded by someone who was very close to him. But one way or another, we associate the book with him, and we are grateful.

Tradition says that Matthew preached in Ethiopia for a time, and also Persia, Parthia, and Macedonia. He died a martyr, as did nearly all the other apostles, perhaps by the sword and perhaps by burning. But the apostolic symbol for Matthew is not the symbol of his martyrdom, but a symbol of what he was when Jesus found him: three money bags, to speak of his past as a tax collector.

And that brings us back to the defining quality of Matthew's life. He was a man of wealth and of economic security when Jesus called him, and he left it all to become a disciple. Because, you see, material accumulation can never fully satisfy us. Money, and the things it can buy, can distract us, can make life more comfortable, and can even give us a measure of power. But it can't fully and profoundly satisfy. As the philosopher has said, there is in each of us a God-shaped void and only God can fill it.

Nevertheless, it's possible to become so absorbed in the

paraphernalia of success that we drown out the voice of God. It could have happened to Matthew. The flow of human traffic, the sounds of the marketplace, the struggle to keep a step ahead of other people, the exhilaration of winning, the excitement of accumulating still more—all of these could have captured Matthew's attention so that he might have missed Jesus' call.

Suppose, on that day when Jesus called him, Matthew had looked a moment longer at what he was giving up, and suppose he had stayed with his prosperous and profitable business; what then? Let's imagine him in his sixties, retired now in a lovely home by the seashore. He is still despised, of course, by his neighbors, because they know how he got his money, but they put up with him more gracefully. He has friends still from the circle of his own kind, and his surroundings are obviously very comfortable.

Now let's ask him a question. "Pardon me for just a moment. What have you done with your life?" Matthew replies with an expansive gesture. "It's quite easy to see. I've succeeded very well. Those who used to resent me still have to pay me credit for what I've done. You can see that I'm comfortable."

"And what will you leave behind? Have you changed any lives for the better, performed any deeds of divine kindness? Or, if I may dare ask such a thing, have you saved any souls? What have you done that matters—really matters?"

Matthew's story doesn't end in a pleasant seaside villa. In fact, it hasn't ended yet. He was martyred, but his name, his writings, and his influence live on, and *will* live on, through all of eternity. So the evangelist in me appeals: Executive, doctor, lawyer, teacher, shopkeeper, secretary, homemaker, delivery person—do your job well, and succeed as honorably and magnificently as you can. Win gloriously in your battles, and I shall rejoice with you. But remember that there is no achievement in life that really matters unless it can pass the bar of eternity, and no success that succeeds unless it is honorable in God's sight. And especially, there is no accumulating that matters, or that lasts, except goodness, kindness, and mercy.

I think Matthew would want to say that to you and to me, Matthew, who gladly traded his measure of human success in order to win Christ and the kingdom of heaven.

CHAPTER 9

$\mathcal{T}$HOMAS, TWENTY-FIRST-CENTURY MAN

READ JOHN 20:19-29.

In some ways, we human beings are the same in every century. We're creatures who need food, rest, and shelter to survive, and who need love, ideas, and communion with others and with God in order to feel our worth. At our worst, we're hardly different from a rapacious animal, but at our best we are only a little lower than the angels. And so it is in every century, for as long as our race has endured.

But in another way, we are always like the times in which we live—almost to the point of being captive of our times. As we read the stories of the apostles, we readily recognize that they were pretty much typical first-century people, except for the passion with which eventually they followed Christ. But there was one who might have fit better in our century—or, for that matter, in any century since perhaps the eighteenth. His name was Thomas.

Which is to say that Thomas had an essentially scientific turn of mind. Most of us have been conditioned that way by our times; Thomas seems to have come by it instinctively, by temperament. Mind you, the first-century world of the disciples wasn't as primitive as we like to think; intellectual myopia afflicts every generation to some degree, but it has reached its most dramatic form in our times, partly because of our accelerated progress in certain fields, and partly because of our faulty knowledge of history. The first-century world had books and scholars, and it may be that their philosophers were superior to ours. But they had no printing presses, to say nothing of computers, so it was difficult to spread knowledge, and their mechanical equipment was primitive, which limited the methodology of research.

As a result, most people in the first-century world had to be satisfied with simple explanations for life's mysteries. We say they were superstitious (we who keep small armies of astrologers in business), but in truth, they were simply making use of the best information they had, and when information ran out, they applied a mixture of imagination and awe. On the other hand, we twenty-first-century people have become so conditioned to science and its methods that we probably don't use insight and intuition as much as we ought. Some future generation will probably think us as superstitious in our own way as were the people of the first century.

In any event, the prevalence and importance of science have had a dramatic impact on our whole twenty-first century way of looking at life. We are cautious to call something a miracle; we're more skeptical, more demanding of proof. Science has trained us to ask appropriate questions, to the point, in fact, where we sometimes ask them in inappropriate places. We want evidence; we want to be sure that studies have been made, and that they have been properly controlled and observed. We're concerned about objectivity and the prejudices of the researchers.

I think Thomas was that kind of person. He was a twenty-first-century man, even though he lived in the first century; just as, I suppose, some of us living in the twenty-first century would be more at home in the late nineteenth century or in the Middle Ages (except for the plumbing!). Thomas had the mind-set of a modern or postmodern person; he could believe a thing only after all the facts were in. He looked not for hopes or dreams or poetry, but for facts, observable facts.

I'm glad there was someone like Thomas among the twelve apostles. We moderns and postmoderns are easily inclined to look upon even the best minds of other centuries as being somehow rather primitive and naïve, so it's very easy to discredit the disciples as quite simple, unscientific souls. But you can't do this with Thomas. You have to recognize that whatever conclusions he finally reached would be by the process of his own standards of rigid testing.

We know almost nothing about Thomas's background. His name is a transliteration of the Aramaic word for "twin." In other words, *Thomas* may not have been a name, but only a nickname. And we're not told who his twin was.

Thomas makes three significant solo appearances in the New Testament story, and they are all recorded in the Gospel of John. As I see it, all three are consistent with the delineation of character that has given him the name "Doubting Thomas," and this has persuaded me to see him as a twenty-first-century person.

In the first instance, Jesus and his disciples were preparing to go to Bethany to pray for Lazarus, who was sick. Some of the disciples objected to the trip, however, because they felt Jesus would be endangering his life by returning to a hostile area. Jesus then told the disciples that Lazarus was already dead, but that he wanted nevertheless to go to him. At this point, Thomas spoke up; in fact, Thomas is the only disciple mentioned by name in this particular story. "Let us also go," Thomas said, "that we may die with him" (John 11:16).

Some Bible students feel that Thomas was showing heroism by this speech—that, recognizing that Jesus might be killed, he was declaring his readiness to be killed with him. I may sound cynical, but I don't see it that way. Having been told by Jesus that Lazarus was dead but that they were going to see him anyway, I hear Thomas saying, in sardonic resignation, "Everything's lost anyway. Let's join dead Lazarus."

But it doesn't matter too much whether you interpret Thomas's words as I have or as the others have; even at best, Thomas comes out as a bit of a pessimist. He's inclined to expect the worst. I see him doing so with a shrug of the shoulders (which may be its own kind of heroism), but others see clenched-fist loyalty in Thomas's words.

Our second experience with Thomas comes during the Last Supper. It was the night before the Crucifixion; specifically, it was only hours before Jesus would be arrested and brought to trial. John's Gospel reports a lengthy statement from Jesus—nothing less than a farewell address. Jesus told the disciples that he was going to prepare a place for them. "And if I go and prepare a place for you, I will come again and take you to myself, so that where I am, there you may be also. And you know the way to the place where I am going" (John 14:3-4).

If I had been there, I would have been taken by the poetic beauty of Jesus' statement, and I would have been afraid to break the spell of the moment. Besides, I would probably have hesitated to confess my ignorance. When someone tells me I know the way somewhere, I agree pleasantly, then begin to worry about getting lost. Not Thomas; not the practical, scientific man. He interrupted immediately. Like any good scholar who realizes the teacher is assuming he knows something that he does not, Thomas raised a question. "Lord, we do not know where you are going. How can we know the way?" (John 14:5).

In that circle of disciples, I see Thomas leaning forward a little farther than the rest, often with a quizzical expression on his face, making sure he really understands what the Master is saying. So when Jesus says, "You know where I'm going, and you know the way," Thomas is quick to say, "Just wait a minute, Sir; I have no idea where you're going, so how can I hope to find my way there?"

Jesus answered Thomas in a philosophical way, but nevertheless to the point. "I am the way, and the truth, and the life. No one comes to the Father except through me" (John 14:6). Nearly twenty centuries of believers have found strength in these words from our Lord. It was Thomas, the questioner, who elicited such a statement.

The third story involving Thomas is the one for which he is best known; it's the one that has given him the popular name "Doubting Thomas"—a phrase, in fact, that has become so much a part of our common speech that many people who use it have no idea from whence it came, or who Thomas was. The title, incidentally, isn't entirely fair, but probably most of us find it somehow perversely encouraging.

Here's how it happened. Near the end of the first Easter day, the disciples were gathered in a private home somewhere. Several of them had seen Jesus that morning, but now they were huddled in a circle of fear and uncertainty. They knew the law might well apprehend them at any moment. They did not fully understand what had happened to Jesus. He had told them on several occasions that he would be crucified and that he would rise again, but somehow they hadn't really processed this information. As they shared, and no doubt reminisced, Jesus suddenly appeared among them, in spite of the locked doors. He showed them the wounds in his hands and his side, and he talked with them, and then he was gone.

But Thomas wasn't there at the time. At times of grief, some people seek the comfort of companions, while others seek the painful beauty of solitude. I think Thomas was in this latter category; this, too, is consistent with what I perceive his personality to be.

Probably he should have been with the others. By temperament, I am myself a bit inclined to Thomas's way; at a time like this, I might also have sought solitude. Nevertheless, I expect Thomas would have been better off, under the circumstances, to have been with the others. We need the company of the faithful, to bear one another's burdens and to rejoice and be strengthened by one another's faith.

Of course it didn't take the others long to report to Thomas. "Did you ever *miss* it, Old Buddy! *We* saw the *Lord!*" Thomas answered with a scholar's exactness. "Unless I see the mark of the nails in his hands, and put my finger in the mark of the nails and my hand in his side, I will not believe" (John 20:25). Thomas wanted to see the proof. Absolute proof. No second-hand research would satisfy him.

At first hearing, Thomas's language may repel us. To put a finger in the mark of the nails, or a hand at the place in the side where the spear had been, sounds almost ghoulish. But we need to remember the events that compelled this language. It was an intensely emotional time for all of the followers of Jesus. I'm sure they were grasping for hope—and, indeed, for any insight or experience that would bring sense into a series of events that seemed utterly senseless. Now Thomas learned that his colleagues have gotten just such an experience, and that he has missed it. His dramatic words are those of a person who is devastated that he has missed the event he needed most, while others have experienced it.

And at the same time, I suspect there's an element of anger and perhaps even of resentment in Thomas. The report of Jesus' appearance to the larger group said that he showed them his hands and his side, the dramatic identification of his wounds. When the group reported to Thomas, I'm sure they included all of these details. And Thomas, feeling the disappointment and latent resentment of someone who has been left out, responded with strong language. I think I catch this tone: "I not only will have to *see* what the rest of you saw, I'll have to put my hands physically on the evidence." One of the wonders of our gospel of grace is that God does not scorn or condemn our honest doubts, any more than God rejects us for our sins.

Eight days passed by (what long days they must have been for Thomas!), and again the disciples were together. This time Thomas was with them. If I may say so, I doubt that he ever absented himself from their company during those eight days!

And again, Jesus suddenly appeared. After an initial greeting to the group, Jesus addressed himself singularly to Thomas: "Put your finger here and see my hands. Reach out your hand and put it in my side. Do not doubt but believe" (John 20:27). There's no indication that Thomas accepted the offer. Instead, he responded with the ultimate language of believing: "My Lord and my God!" (John 20:28). Thomas had stumbled (as scholars often do) upon the answer to his research, and with the humility of an honorable student, he bowed in reverence before the facts. But of course facts alone are never enough for a commitment of life; Thomas had also experienced faith, and with the awe of a newborn believer, he bowed before his Lord in discipleship.

Jesus then spoke a word for all of the rest of us believers: "Have you believed because you have seen me? Blessed are those who have not seen and yet have come to believe" (John 20:29).

According to the most reliable traditions, Thomas preached through much of Asia (some say, even, that he went to China), and especially that he preached in India. At any rate, when Vasco da Gama and his Portugese explorers arrived in India around A.D. 1500, they found a church there that identified itself as the Christians of Saint Thomas; and a sixth-century book tells us that a traveler in India found a church in Malabar, as well as a bishop in Galiana, south of Bombay. According to tradition, Thomas died a martyr's death in a suburb of Madras, on a mountain that now bears the name Mount Thomas. His death came by the piercing of a lance—thus the symbol of Thomas is the lance, for his martyrdom, and a carpenter's triangle, since he was supposedly a builder by trade.

A major body in India has for centuries carried Thomas's name, the Mar Thoma Church. Thomas is the only disciple to have a denomination named for him. And perhaps it is significant that this church, named for Thomas, has proved outstanding for its fidelity and its great courage.

Thomas lived, struggled, and preached in the first century, but I'm satisfied that he would be at home in the twenty-first. In our day, Jesus would probably find Thomas in the physics or chemistry department of a university, or perhaps in some independent think tank. He was a man who looked for the facts, always insisting on substantial evidence.

So it's impressive that he left us with what may well be the most vigorous and committed confession of faith to be found anywhere in the New Testament: *My Lord and my God!*

Perhaps our twenty-first-century world—this generation so possessed of the spirit of Thomas—will yet come to be the greatest generation of faith. Please, God, may it be so!

CHAPTER 10
$\mathcal{T}$HADDAEUS, THE QUESTIONER

READ JOHN 14:18-24.

When we start naming the apostles, most of us find it hard to remember Thaddaeus. His name isn't a common one in our day; in fact, I doubt that it ever has been. He seems to have had only a minor role among the apostles. Then, to complicate matters still more, he is known by three different names in the New Testament, so it's easy to miss him or confuse him; he sometimes is called Thaddaeus, sometimes Lebbaeus, and sometimes Judas (Mark 3:18; Matthew 10:3 in KJV and certain other translations; Luke 6:16).

In truth, we have good reason to think that this disciple's true name was Judas. But what would you do if you were a disciple of Jesus Christ, and your name was Judas? In a body where the name Judas Iscariot must have taken on the quality of an evil omen, it's likely that Thaddaeus did what you or I probably would have done. And it's likely that his friends helped, by using his other names as often as possible. When the Gospel of John mentioned him by the name Judas, it hurries to add "not Iscariot" (John 14:22).

I have tried, in this study of the apostles, not to emphasize the legends that have grown around them. Most of the legends would be hard to prove from a historical point of view, so I've reasoned that their value lies mainly in quaintness and speculation.

But I want to tell you a story about Thaddaeus, simply

because it's such a beautiful, gently sentimental thing. According to this legend, Thaddaeus (or Jude) was a little boy who worked with shepherds near Bethlehem. He was too young to watch over the sheep, but he ran errands for the older shepherds. When the angels announced to the shepherds that the Christ Child had been born, little Jude was on the scene, and he followed the other shepherds to see the newborn baby.

According to the ancient story, the boy stayed on for a few moments after the older shepherds had left, because he was captivated by the beauty of the child. Seeing the love in the boy's eyes, the mother Mary laid the baby in his arms for a moment. Thirty years later, the boy Jude, now a man approaching forty, was chosen by Jesus to be one of the Twelve. Such is the legend that has grown around Thaddaeus, or Jude. It may be true or it may not. It's possible, of course, that something similar to this happened that gave rise to the legend itself. It's a lovely story in its own right, the kind of story all of us like to attach to the more substantial data of the Gospel accounts. At the least, it demonstrates the affection with which early believers built a structure of adoration around their Lord.

Thaddaeus is another of the inconspicuous disciples. He's one of those persons who fade into the background; after a social gathering, your spouse might ask, "Did you notice if Thaddaeus was there?" and you would reply after a moment, "I really can't say; I just didn't notice." We know very little about Thaddaeus. But that's true about so many of the Twelve. And this is part of what I hope we'll grasp as we study their lives. First, that our Lord laid hold of all kinds and varieties of persons to do the Kingdom's work, and second, that a good percentage of those people were average human beings.

But let me hasten to say that *average* ought not to mean "mediocre." "Average" is a measure of comparison to others' talents, while "mediocre" is a measure of what we do with our-selves. Remember that in sports the difference between "aver-age" and "champion" is only a matter of seconds, or even of tenths of seconds; and in the measure of life, the difference between "average" and "historic" is only an accumulation of relatively small decisions. This is partly to say that the mean-ing of *average* is difficult to determine, so we ought to use the term cautiously; and still more, that we ought never to mini-mize our own role or potential, because we may not know how close we are to being a key component in eternity's unfolding.

Some years ago Kirk M. Reid, a retired corporate executive, wrote a short dramatic story about the twelve apostles, and he kindly shared a copy with me. He imagined them as an exec-utive might, appearing before a screening committee made up of expert personnel managers. As the committee evaluates the data pulled up by their computers and reflects upon their observations, they find that not one of the candidates is really qualified for a position of major trust. And as for our man Thaddaeus, Mr. Reid doesn't even treat him individually; true to our observation, he makes him one of a group of four who receive a kind of group interview, of whom the screening com-mittee reports, "These four are just average, or perhaps below-average, men. No special abilities, no speaking or teaching experience, little or no leadership potential" (*Fishers of Men*, Educational Research Council of America, 1974; page 11).

I suspect Mr. Reid had a point. If someone should ask you to name the twelve apostles, how far would you get? Farther, I hope, after you've read this book! But short of that, or the memorizing of some childhood rhyme, a good many of us would settle for Peter, James, and John, with Judas Iscariot coming in for unfortunate reasons, and perhaps Thomas by way of his notable doubtings. After that, it gets difficult. And perhaps that's the best proof that Jesus worked with ordinary material. Peter, James, and John were probably what we would call "born leaders," though I expect that they are the kind of persons, potentially, that we might find on any small-town board of education or serving a term in a service-club presidency. Matthew must have been a person of above-average abilities, as we've already observed, and Judas Iscariot and Thomas no doubt had real potential. But the other names fade into a haze of anonymity. Apparently they were generally ordinary human beings—and with such as these, our Lord chose to lay a foundation for an eternal work.

I hate to say the obvious, but there's a lesson here for us. The contemporary church is sometimes tempted to pour everyone into a common mold. In some cases it's our inclination to surround ourselves with "our kind of people," the sort of folk whose children we want our children to marry. In other instances, the church consultants do it for us; their studies conclude that a certain type of music, preaching, or worship pattern is the new hope of the church, and wittingly or unwittingly they leave the impression that *everyone* should be included in this typing.

But Jesus didn't operate this way. In his little band of twelve he brought together a remarkable variety of talents, temperaments, and levels of capacity. Later, the apostle Paul compared the Christian church to the human body, with every body part having its own peculiar function. Paul could have illustrated his point by pointing to the original apostles. But of course he didn't need to, because he had such wondrous variety within his own congregations.

Thaddaeus is singled out for attention only once in the biblical story, and then it is for a question he asked. If the only thing we know about Thaddaeus is that he asked questions, let it be said that this is a special kind of commendation. The person who asks questions can be like the person who throws on a light switch in a dark room. It's by questioning that knowledge is gained and ignorance dispelled.

But a person will ask good questions only if he has a happy combination of intelligence and humility. Intelligence is essential, because one has to have a certain amount of insight in order to ask worthwhile questions. I've found that I know so little in some areas of knowledge that I can't even frame questions. Humility is necessary, because the asking of questions is a confession not only that there are some things I don't know, but also that I acknowledge that you are far enough ahead of me to know these very things. Of course, I'm speaking of true questions. All of us have observed those cases where someone makes a little speech or throws out to the speaker a challenge masquerading as a question. In such instances, the interrogator is trying to make a point, not seeking information.

Thaddaeus was apparently a big enough human being to ask questions. Mind you, it may be only by chance that his one recorded statement is a question. But on the other hand, perhaps the reason the Gospel records this instance is because it is so typical of Thaddaeus.

His question came during Jesus' last evening with his disciples before his crucifixion. Jesus was explaining that he was going to send them the Spirit of Truth, who, he said, the world would not receive. This apparently troubled Thaddaeus, as perhaps it troubled others around the table. Thaddaeus probably expected (as did all the disciples) that Jesus would set up his kingdom at that very time, so he wondered why Jesus would say that most people would not accept what he was saying. So Thaddaeus asked Jesus, "Lord, how is it that you will reveal yourself to us, and not to the world?" (John 14:22).

It was an appropriate question. Thaddaeus (and his colleagues) must have wondered why Jesus wasn't promoting his cause with a full-scale campaign. It was time, to put it in our vernacular, for a full-court press, with plenty of advertising, establishing a public image, and solidifying popular support.

Why, at this time, was Jesus making such defeatist talk? And if one major traditional belief about Thaddaeus is true, that he was a Zealot, the logic of his question would be all the more insistent. The Zealots, as I noted in our study of Simon (chapter 6), were a revolutionary political movement. If Thaddaeus really was a Zealot, he had to be completely bewildered and upset by what he saw as Jesus' strategy.

The answer Jesus gave could easily have frustrated him still more. "Those who love me will keep my word, and my Father will love them, and we will come to them and make our home with them. Whoever does not love me does not keep my words" (John 14:23-24).

With those few words, Jesus stated the operating principle of his kingdom. It is a kingdom of love, and it is ultimately useless to try to promote it any other way. Thaddaeus must have wanted to know why Jesus wouldn't dazzle the crowds into joining the cause; indeed, if Thaddaeus was a Zealot, he might have wondered why Jesus didn't employ some of his obvious power to bring the crowds under his control. Jesus explained that a person cannot be forced into discipleship. If we are going to follow Jesus' teachings, it will be because we love him. As Jesus said, in the words of the J. B. Phillips translation, "The man who does not really love Me will not follow My teaching."

This is a correction for so many of our missionary and evangelistic endeavors. Constantine and a good many later military and government leaders believed they could make Christians by force; the sword convinced one to accept baptism! Generations of earnest parents and clergy have tried to make Christians by fiat: Require young people to fulfill certain rituals and ecclesiastical requirements, and they will be saved. Others have placed their hopes on education: Give children an effective catechism, and they will graduate as Christians. Just now the favorite approach is a combination of popular psychology, fast-paced entertainment, and high-powered promotion.

But Jesus' answer to Thaddaeus applies as well to all our subsequent theories and practices: *When someone loves me, he or she follows my teaching.* No one who does not really love Christ will follow his teachings. You can hold a threat over a person's head until they're baptized; you can make someone learn a doctrine or a set of Bible passages until they can pass a religious intelligence test; you can promote religion with the most advanced and persuasive electronic gimmicks until someone is seduced into signing on the dotted line. But you can't make *disciples* by any of these means.

Mind you, many of these elements, rightly used, have their place. We should, of course, educate, and we should be as able and progressive as possible in the use of every effective resource. But in the end, people come to follow the teaching of Christ, and to accept his demanding claim, because they love him. We're dealing with an individual act of heart and will. The kingdom of Christ is a kingdom of love, and we enter this kingdom through the doorway of earnest devotion.

The Bible makes one other reference to Thaddaeus—this time again by the name Judas—when it lists those who were with Jesus at the time of his ascension, and who then returned to Jerusalem to wait for the outpouring of the Holy Spirit (Acts 1:13). After that, Thaddaeus never reappears in the biblical account.

But legend and tradition say that he traveled to Edessa, where he worked a miraculous healing for the king, Abgar, which resulted in the king's conversion. Thaddaeus is also supposed to have preached in Persia and Armenia. His ministry is said to have ended in martyrdom, after much torture, from the wounds of arrows.

When most of us think of Thaddaeus, however, it's probably by the name Jude, the shortened form for Judas.

Protestants almost as well as Catholics have become conversant with Saint Jude through the work of the late entertainer and comedian Danny Thomas, who established a special healing facility in Memphis, Tennessee, in the name of Saint Jude. This name was chosen because Saint Jude—Thaddaeus—is known in the Roman tradition as the patron saint of the desperate and the despairing, the saint of lost causes.

And of course there's a story behind that. Since he bore the same name as the betrayer, Judas Iscariot, Thaddaeus—Judas—suffered a burden of identity with many early Christians. Those who prayed through the saints were reluctant to use Judas's name as their advocate, unless and until all other saints had been appealed to without success. Thus Jude became the saint of last resort. And (what a delightful twist!) the name that must have burdened this man during much of his adult life, so that he gladly accepted Thaddaeus or Lebbaeus, has become for many a beloved name in their hour of extremity.

I have called him "the Questioner," in recognition of his one moment of singular identity in the New Testament story. Some, who have found themselves driven into one of life's impossible and hopeless corners, love him as the symbol of faith's last desperate reach for an answer. That's a high and lovely achievement for a person who had to live with a bad name.

CHAPTER 11

*J*UDAS, THE VALUE OF A DOLLAR

READ JOHN 13:21-30.

Judas Iscariot, the disciple who betrayed Jesus, fascinates us. Some of us might confess that we find him the most intriguing of all the disciples. He is the accident we pass on the highway, to which our eyes are drawn even as we prepare to be repelled by what we see.

Perhaps it's the rule of drama that finds villains more interesting than heroes. Most novelists confess that they'd rather develop their bad characters than their good ones, because it's so difficult to make the good ones interesting. I wonder if this is because there's a little of the villain in every one of us, so when we watch the villain in action we see some elements of our own character, slightly or largely magnified? Most of us are wise enough to know, when we pass a derelict soul, that it is "there, but for the grace of God, go I." So when we look at someone who has done a quite monstrous thing, we ask ourselves how it is that he or she came to such a place—and perhaps, sometimes, how it is that we did not.

What made Judas do what he did? What circumstances, what mounting influence, or what subliminal darkness in his heritage made Judas do what I fear I'm capable of doing, but yet have never done?

As dramatically evil as is Judas's act of betraying Jesus, most of us feel some measure of sympathy for him. Some people feel that Judas didn't get a fair break. After all, the Christian faith declares that Jesus was crucified as part of the divine plan for the salvation of our human race. If that be so, wasn't Judas essential to the unfolding of the plan? Was he, in fact, a kind of divine catalyst? Some have even said that perhaps he should be praised for fulfilling the ugliest of roles in this eternal drama.

Jesus himself spoke to the question. "For the Son of Man goes as it is written of him, but woe to that one by whom the Son of Man is betrayed!" (Mark 14:21). One thinks also of Jesus saying to his disciples at another time, "Occasions for stumbling are bound to come, but woe to anyone by whom they come!" (Luke 17:1). I think Jesus is telling us, in very pragmatic fashion, that in a world of sin many tragedies will happen; but each person can decide for himself or herself whether or not to be the instrument of tragedy.

I have great sympathy for Judas, not only because he is a pathetic figure, but because the seed of divine betrayal is in each of us. And while I really cannot imagine myself performing the Judas-deed, I know my capacity for my own kinds of shame and betrayal. Nevertheless, I don't believe Judas was helpless; I don't believe he was simply a divine pawn. I believe he could have resisted evil, and that he could have been a disciple of honor, with his story continuing into the book of Acts, and on into legend and tradition.

So why did Judas do it? You remember the story. Judas Iscariot was one of the disciples, a person chosen by Jesus as a leader. He was part of that small and uniquely blessed group who lived with the Master day and night for perhaps three years, sharing in our Lord's struggles and triumphs, and feeding daily on his teachings. Then one day he slipped away from the disciples to drive a bargain with the enemies of Jesus.

Judas had heard that the chief priests and scribes were looking for a way to be rid of Jesus. He went to them and settled on a means of getting Jesus into their hands quietly. They agreed on a price, and the deal was closed.

Sometime later, the disciples gathered with Jesus in an upper room, to celebrate the Passover. In the course of the meal, Jesus said that one of the little group would betray him. It was an astonishing statement, quite beyond belief. But the disciples responded in a remarkable way: Each one asked, with obvious anxiety, "Lord, is it I?" (Matthew 26:22 KJV). Whatever immaturities they may have shown at other times, at this moment they were spiritual enough to recognize their personal frailty and their capacity for sin.

Jesus and Judas then had a brief conversation, and Judas left the room. Since Judas was treasurer of the disciples, the others assumed that he was going out to buy additional supplies or perhaps to do something for the poor. Not long afterward, Jesus and the remaining disciples went to the Garden of Gethsemane, where Jesus prayed. It was without doubt the most significant prayer offered in the history of our human race. As the group prepared to leave the garden, a band of soldiers appeared, with Judas among them. The moon was full, providing quite good vision, but to prevent the possibility of error, Judas had arranged a signal that would identify Jesus to the soldiers, so the arrest could be made expeditiously. He chose a practical signal; in those days, disciples customarily greeted their teachers by placing hands on the rabbi's shoulders and kissing him.

So Judas had said, "The one I will kiss is the man; arrest him" (Matthew 26:48). One would expect that a betrayal kiss would be as brief and uninvolving as possible, but in the Gospels of Matthew and Mark, the Greek word *kataphilein* is used—a word that means to kiss fondly and repeatedly. Why did Judas kiss his Lord with such intensity? Was it only to heighten the irony of his signal? Or was it because, once he faced his Lord, he was overwhelmed by the terror of his deed and by his latent devotion to his Master?

The authorities quickly took Jesus to trial, persecuted him, and crucified him. And Judas was the catalyst in the story, making his name forever afterward the classic synonym for *traitor*. What made him do it?

I venture that thousands of artists—some of them classic practitioners and vast others unknown—have painted pictures of Judas. As I said earlier, he fascinates us. Always, of course, the artists try to show the evil in his face. But he didn't start life as an evil human being, any more than any of the rest of us. Once, he was somebody's baby, a helpless, lovely thing that a mother cuddled and a father juggled proudly in the air.

I use such language with some assurance, because his parents gave him an honored, beautiful name, *Judah* or *Judas*. In those days, a Jewish boy could have no finer name. It had a jubilant, spiritual tone, meaning "praise to God." This was the name of one of the twelve sons of Jacob (Israel), and the name of the greatest tribe, the one from which King David came. It was the name also of Judas Maccabaeus, the great Jewish hero, and of Judas of Galilee, another hero, from the generation just preceding. Jewish parents of the first century could hardly speak a higher hope for a child than to name him Judah or Judas.

No one can prove all that is in a name, but I've long noticed that we tend to live up—or down—to the name we are given. Give a girl a name with intimations of beauty, and she is likely to lay claim to it; give a boy a "real boy" name, and he generally embodies it. So Judas grew up with a great name, and perhaps with equally great expectations. Then, somewhere in his young manhood, he met the challenging young teacher from Nazareth. He listened to Jesus, and gave him his heart.

Mind you, I fully believe that Judas gave Jesus his heart. I don't feel that he was a tentative follower. No doubt he joined Jesus with mixed motives; I'm fully convinced that we human beings rarely if ever do things with utterly pure motives. But I believe Judas joined Jesus' band with sincere, devout commit-ment—as good, I venture, as any other of the disciples.

Jesus seems to have received Judas with high expectations. Judas was clearly a capable man, and he got a place of leader-ship among the Twelve. Specifically, he was held in such trust that he was made treasurer of the group—a tribute to both his judgment and his evidences of integrity.

And there's more. At the Last Supper, John's Gospel gives us the impression that Judas was seated in the position of the most favored guest, at the Master's left, because Jesus handed the sop (the dipped bread) to Judas, and at a Passover feast for the host to make up the sop and hand it to a guest was a mark of particular honor. It's also clear that Judas was seated near enough to Jesus that they were able to carry on a quite private conversation.

Yet Judas became the traitor. Why did he do it?

Some try to justify Judas's deed by reasoning that Judas didn't really intend to betray Jesus, but that he wanted only to force him to act. They say that Judas, too, was a Zealot—there is tradition to this effect—and that Judas felt the time had come for Jesus to organize his revolution. According to this theory, Judas believed that if Jesus were arrested, he would be forced to commit himself, and the revolution would begin. This is an ingenious defense of Judas, but it depends almost entirely on imagination. There's no real support for it in the record of the Scriptures.

Others have found an interesting theory in Judas's surname. "Iscariot" suggests that Judas came from Kerioth in Judea. This would mean that Judas was the only Judean among the disci-ples; all the others were Galileans. The Judeans spoke a dif-ferent dialect and were a stricter people than the Galileans. Perhaps Judas felt shut out because of the difference in lan-guage, customs, and tradition, especially since he was the only one of his kind in the group. It's very easy for a loner to become antisocial and bitter if he or she doesn't take care. This seems to me to be a possible contributing factor in Judas's story, but I don't think it is a major issue.

From what I understand of human personality and of the principle of sin, I think the important issue in Judas is that of strength and weakness. Always speak of a person's strength and weakness in the same breath, for most likely they are opposite sides of the same coin. As someone has wisely noted, "Temptation commonly comes through that for which we are naturally fitted."

It does, indeed. In this regard, the story of Judas is the story of all of us. If a person's strength is a fine mind, the Waterloo will be at the issue of the mind. If personality is the strength, it will almost as surely be the peril. Is a person impressive for disciplined habits? Then know that discipline itself may some-day be the point of downfall. We are more likely to destroy our souls at the height of our talent than at the level of our ordinariness.

So what was Judas's strength? Pretty clearly this: that he handled money well. To use a phrase from our common speech, he knew the value of a dollar. No doubt that's why he was made treasurer of the disciples. This was a significant compliment. After all, Matthew was a tax collector, a person who dealt all the time in money, and most of the rest of the group were small businessmen, people instinctively proud of their ability to make good use of limited resources. Yet it was in such a group that Judas's ability with money was recognized as so outstanding that he was chosen as treasurer.

But if handling money was Judas's strength, it was even more dramatically his weakness. The evidence is painful and inescapable. The point is implied in Matthew's Gospel (26:6-16) and plainly stated in John's (12:1-11). As Matthew tells the story, an unnamed woman interrupted a meal where Jesus was a guest and poured a very expensive perfume on him. The disciples "were angry" because of her wastefulness. Jesus, however, rebuked the disciples, explaining that the woman had done a deed of sincere devotion, and that her act was a preparing of his body for burial. Matthew goes on immediately to say, "Then one of the twelve, who was called Judas Iscariot, went to the chief priests and said, 'What will you give me if I betray him to you?'" (Matthew 26:14-15). I think there is no doubt that Matthew sees the anointing event as the act that impels Judas to his work of betrayal. As Matthew says, it was "then," after the bitter incident, and resulting from it, that Judas went into action.

John, as I said, is more direct. As he tells the story, it was Mary, sister of Martha and Lazarus, who anointed Jesus with the expensive perfume; and it was not just the disciples in general who objected, it was Judas in particular. Putting the two accounts together, I suspect that all the disciples murmured, but Judas gave specific voice to their feelings. He was true to his skills; he knew the value of the ointment, and he calculated what could be done with such a sum. It could have been sold, he said, "for three hundred denarii and the money given to the poor." Since a *denarii* was a day's wages for a laboring man, this ointment represented essentially a year of a laborer's wages.

But John's Gospel doesn't let the matter lie there; it adds an editorial comment. Judas said what he did, John tells us, not because he cared for the poor, "but because he was a thief; he kept the common purse and used to steal what was put into it" (12:6).

Whatever case one wants to make for Judas (and I am sympathetic, because Judas and all humanity and I are kin), certain facts seem to me to be compelling. Judas was fascinated by money and was stealing from the apostolic purse. So when he was rebuked by Jesus, he went out to betray him. It seems to me that John's Gospel is telling us that Judas's act of betrayal had antecedents, as do all of our deeds, both good and bad. The betrayal had its conception in a love of money, and it got its final impetus in the scene of anointing. On that occasion, perhaps two things happened. For one, Judas saw again how "unrealistic" Jesus was in his values; what hope could there be for a leader who saw things as Jesus did? Then, the rebuke. When we are corrected, whether by parent, teacher, spouse, friend, or foe, we can learn from it or we can turn angry and inward. Judas did the latter.

So he sold his Master for thirty pieces of silver. There's irony in the sum; this was the going price, in those days, for a slave. It was a pathetic, tragic bargain—the kind of bargain that would be driven only by someone who knew the value of a dollar. It is always at the point of our strength that we are most susceptible to error, and at the peak of our ability that we are most in danger of destroying ourselves.

What is the end of Judas's story? The New Testament gives two reports (Matthew 27:3-10; Acts 1:16-20), but I think they are nothing other than varying insights on the same data. When Judas realized what he had done, he hurried to the priests to see if he might call off the whole, bad bargain. They laughed at his appeal. Judas then threw the thirty pieces of silver to the ground at their feet. At last, at last, Judas was getting his values straight. But not quite. Because then he went out and hanged himself.

I hurt with Judas in his remorse. Many of the things we do wrong can somehow be made right. But now and again we take steps that can never on this earth be retraced. Of this I'm sure: Judas should have gone to Jesus with his remorse, for it was against Jesus that he had sinned. Even if Jesus were already on the cross, Judas should have clung to the tree in loving sorrow. And as Christian theology understands it, Judas needed most of all to understand that his sins were not dealt with by hanging himself, but by trusting the One who was dying in his stead at Golgotha.

And this brings us to a question over which people have speculated since the first century: Was Judas lost? Or will we see him in heaven? George MacDonald, the nineteenth-century novelist (of whom C. S. Lewis said, "I regarded him as my master" because of his closeness to the Spirit of Christ), said in his *Unspoken Sermons*, "I think, when Judas fled from his hanged and fallen body, he fled to the tender help of Jesus, and found it—I say not how" (quoted in *The Wind from the Stars*, Gordon Reid, editor, HarperCollins, 1992; page 173). Origen, the third-century philosopher and theologian, found a "how": He said that when Judas realized what he had done, he hurried to commit suicide so that he might meet Jesus in Hades, the abode of the dead, and there bare his soul and seek his Lord's forgiveness (Origen, *Sermons on Matthew*, 35, cited in William Barclay, *The Master's Men*, Abingdon Press, 1959; page 80).

I choose just now to leave the soul of Judas with his God, walking quietly from the place where a human being meets his or her Maker. As I slip away, I remind myself that Judas was a very able human being, and that it was at the point of his strength that he destroyed himself. I will remember that so many of our worst deeds and errors are at the place of our greatest strengths.

Judas helps me to understand some things about myself, and to seek God's mercy and strength. You, too, perhaps?

CHAPTER 12

*J*OHN, LOVE AND THUNDER

READ MARK 9:33-41.

Now and again I get involved in "then and now" conversations. You know what I mean. It may be some men discussing a professional athlete, recalling that he was a low draft choice but is now a star. Sometimes it's a teacher remembering a difficult student who is now everybody's favorite success story. And more than once it has been a parent recalling a daughter who, as a teenager, presided over a room that was a disaster area, but who now (believe it or not!) maintains an immaculate apartment.

That is the kind of conversation I imagine from the Christian church at Ephesus late in the first century. Tradition says that by that time only one of the original disciples was still living, the apostle John, and that by now he was so old and infirm that he couldn't come to worship or teaching gatherings unless the young men carried him. As they would bring the great old man into such gatherings, I think I see the worshipers rising in respect, and parents lifting their children so they can see this venerable saint.

As Saint Jerome reported it several centuries later, on such occasions John would be presented with a lengthy, complimentary preparatory service. Then they would lift him to his feet to speak; and with everyone waiting in awe, John would say, simply, "Little children, love one another, love one another, love one another." And this is where I imagine the "then and now" comment. If by chance someone in the gathering was the child or grandchild of a person who knew John in his earliest days, they would marvel, "And to think that he was once young Fire and Thunder! To think that the Son of Thunder is now the apostle of love!"

Such is the story of John the apostle. He is the young man of thunder who became everyone's favorite example of love.

The Bible tells us a good deal about John, perhaps more than any other apostle, except perhaps Peter. He was the younger brother of the apostle James, as we noted earlier. Like his brother, he was a fisherman by trade, growing up in the home of Zebedee and Salome. While John was still a young man, he became a close friend of another young fisherman, Simon, who was to become known later as Peter.

And while still young, he seems to have begun a lifelong quest for spiritual fulfillment. Like several others in the group that eventually joined Jesus, John first associated himself with another John, John the Baptist. But when John the Baptist pointed one day to the young Galilean, Jesus of Nazareth, and described him as the Lamb of God, young John left the Baptist and followed Jesus.

When I use the term "young John," it is quite deliberate. Tradition says he was probably the youngest of the disciples. Some even suggest that he was still in his teens when he joined the group. When we read, therefore, of some of his conduct, we should remember that John was still in what one bishop used to say was a preacher's "green-apple stage." We may look back on our teenage years romantically, but they're sometimes painful years—especially for those who have to live with us. When I look back on my own life (and sometimes when I ponder the lives of some of my students), I think that the best thing about being young is that we have so much time to repent of it.

But Jesus saw the potential in the young man; so much

potential, in fact, that when he selected an inner circle of persons who would be most closely associated with him, and on whom he would count the most, John was one of the group, along with Peter and James. It was an extraordinary honor for one so young. I venture that it didn't add to John's humility. But of course I'm reflecting on some of my own rather limited experiences.

Early pictures of John are not always pretty. If John is love and thunder, at the outset the thunder is apparent more often. The Gospels of Matthew, Mark, and Luke give us three incidents in which John stars. They reveal him as unattractively ambitious, with something bordering on a violent temper, and with an intolerant heart.

I won't say much about the first two incidents, since I reported them in our story of John's older brother, James (chapter 3). And of course the brothers were cut from the same cloth, so that Jesus described them—perhaps somewhat playfully, but also pointedly—as "sons of thunder." Let me remind you briefly. In the one instance, the disciples learned that a village in Samaria had refused hospitality to Jesus because Jesus was headed for Jerusalem. When James and John heard this, they volunteered to Jesus that they would be glad to call down fire from heaven to destroy the people of that village (Luke 9:51-56). When you see John ready to burn up his enemies, you aren't likely to predict that he will someday be known as the apostle of love. Only the thunder was apparent.

In the second instance, James and John took Jesus aside to ask a special favor: They wanted to be seated on Jesus' right and left hand when he became king (Mark 10:35-45). Again, there is little evidence of loving concern on John's part. His colleagues are easily sacrificed to his own proud ambition. It's clear that they weren't even in his mind, except perhaps as competitors.

John has the center stage to himself in the third story;

James has no part. Once more, he's hardly a noble character. John was reporting to Jesus an incident in which several of the disciples probably had played a part, but it's John who took it upon himself to tell Jesus. "'Teacher, we saw someone casting out demons in your name, and we tried to stop him, because he was not following us'" (Mark 9:38).

I recognize that voice very well. I've heard it often, and probably you have, too. "He may claim to be a Christian, but if he doesn't belong to our church, he can't take Communion with us." "Yes, he's an effective preacher, but he belongs to some offbeat denomination, and he's never seen the inside of a theological seminary." Or, on the other hand, "You know, he really does seem spiritual, but I wouldn't trust somebody who's gone to a seminary."

Such was the spirit of John. "Teacher, we saw someone casting out demons in your name, and *we tried to stop him!*" That's the way to handle it, John. If you see good being done, don't think about the poor soul that's being healed, just ask to see the healer's credentials. Check his affiliations. Be sure he belongs to your religious union. Let the world go to hell unless the work is done by *our* people, according to *our* methods, with *our* group receiving a good share of the credit.

Jesus answered John with both strength and kindness. "Do not stop him; for no one who does a deed of power in my name will be able soon afterward to speak evil of me. Whoever is not against us is for us" (Mark 9:39-40). There is breadth in Jesus' words that seeks to let people in rather than shut them out. It recognizes that not everyone is on our side, and that there are indeed standards to be fulfilled; that some are for Christ and some are against him. And that's surely a factor to be dealt with in our particular culture, which finds it hard to make definitions. But we should not be too quick to shut others out because they don't dot their *i*'s and cross their *t*'s to our satisfaction.

The nineteenth-century poet Frederick W. Faber said it well. Born an Anglican, raised with strong Calvinist theology, he eventually became a devout Roman Catholic. Finding Catholicism lacking in the hymns that had blessed his life as a Protestant, he wrote several hundred hymns that Christians of all persuasions sing today. He knew what he was saying when he wrote:

> For the love of God is broader
>   than the measure of our mind;
> and the heart of the Eternal
>   is most wonderfully kind.
> ("There's a Wideness in God's Mercy," 1854)

Broad as is God's love, however, it is also effective in its definitions. There's a type of sentimentality that is not truly loving, because unless love recognizes the distinction between good and evil, it takes all the goodness out of the good. John meant well when he threw up some institutional barriers, but Jesus corrected those barriers. He didn't destroy them, it seems to me, for lines of definition are necessary, but he interpreted them more generously than John was ready to do. And of course one reason John was more narrow may well have been because he was trying to protect his own turf. Many boundaries that we ascribe to faith-conviction may in truth be self-aggrandizement. Human as we are, it's sometimes difficult to tell the difference.

The Fourth Gospel bears John's name. Some Bible scholars believe it was written by John the apostle, while others feel it was written by someone else who was close to John and who reflected so faithfully John's words and teachings that he had a right to attach John's name to the book. However that may be, it's interesting and no doubt significant that this book tells us little about John by name, but that it refers in a number of crucial instances to "the disciple whom Jesus loved." There is every reason to believe that this is, of course, John himself.

Several particular references come to mind. It was to this disciple that Peter turned when he wanted to find out who the traitor in their group was. It was to this disciple that Jesus entrusted Mary, his mother, at the time of the Crucifixion. It was also this disciple who arrived at the tomb early on Easter morning with Peter. And it was about the future of this particular disciple that Simon Peter inquired when Jesus met with the disciples by the lakeside after the Resurrection (see John 13:21-25; 19:26-27; 20:1-10; 21:20-24).

John's story continues on into the book of Acts; of the original Twelve, only he and Peter get much attention there. John was with Peter when the man who was paralyzed was healed at the gate of the Temple, he was with Peter when they were arrested and brought to trial for preaching, and he went with Peter to Samaria to carry on Philip's revival there. Later, when the new apostle, Paul, listed the great leaders of the Christian church, John's name was on the list (Acts, chapters 3, 4, 8; Galatians 2:9).

So the Bible record ends there, but tradition tells us much more. You remember that Jesus asked from the cross that John would take care of his mother, Mary. Tradition says that John was faithful to this trust, and that he stayed in Jerusalem and cared for her like a son until the day of her death. It also says that he was flung into a cauldron of burning oil, but that he emerged unharmed, and that he was compelled to drink the cup of hemlock, but that it did not affect him.

There is still more. Tradition says that John was banished to the Isle of Patmos, probably in the time of the emperor Domitian, and it was on this island that John had the remarkable experiences, visions, and insights recorded in the book of Revelation. If you visit this island today, tour guides will lead you to traditional sacred spots. When he was liberated from Patmos, tradition continues, John came to Ephesus and there became a revered figure—by that time the only surviving member of the original Twelve.

I mentioned earlier Jerome's great story about the occasions when John, in his old age, would be carried into the gatherings of the church at Ephesus, and how he would simply exhort the group to "love one another." Jerome goes on to say that the leaders at Ephesus grew weary of this same, simple message, and said, "Master, why dost thou always say this?" To which John replied, "It is the Lord's command, and, if this alone be done, it is enough" (Jerome, *Commentary on Galatians*, 6, 10, quoted in William Barclay, *The Master's Men*, Abingdon Press, 1959; page 38).

This is quite a leap from the brash young disciple who said, somewhat hopefully, "Shall we call down fire and destroy them?" and who secretly asked for first place in the Kingdom. And it's surely a different mood from the disciple who reported, "We found someone doing good in your name who wasn't traveling with us, so we stopped him." How is it that the man of thunder became the apostle of love?

One factor, surely, is that John came to Jesus at such an early age. He had time to grow and to be shaped by his Lord. The more malleable the clay, the more the potter can do with it. Probably this is part of what Jesus had in mind when he said that we must become as little children if we are to enter the kingdom of heaven.

A still bigger factor, it seems to me, is the phrase that characterizes John in the Fourth Gospel, identifying him as being especially beloved. It is as we experience love that we learn how to love. The Scripture says, "We love because he [God] first loved us" (1 John 4:19). Every human being has not only a capacity to love, but a very great need to exercise that capacity. But our ability to love has to be set free. If one never experiences love, the ability to love is likely to be frustrated, and at last even destroyed. One of the surest signs of true conversion is a great new feeling of love—love that often includes people who were previously overlooked or even despised and resented. From whence do we get this new love? From the experience of being loved.

The Christian gospel commands us to love our neighbor as we love ourselves. If the gospel did no more than make this command, it would only saddle us with another virtually impossible assignment. Nothing is so hard as to act like a Christian without becoming one; maybe that's why hypocrisy slips in unbidden. To try to love people in grand, indiscriminate fashion is a pretty disheartening task unless we first experience the transforming love of God in our hearts. So here's the good news of the Christian faith: *God loves us*, and because God loves us, we are empowered to love others.

I think this is John's story. By nature, he was a thunderer, someone ready to call down judgment, anxious to push into first place regardless of anyone else's hopes or feelings, and quick to shut others out. But John met love in the person of Jesus Christ, and he lived with Love, until he became the apostle of love. And the glory of his conversion was—as is so often the case—that his newfound love was in the extravagant measure of his former thunder.

But observe that it didn't happen overnight. All of the unpleasant facets of John's personality are reported to us from the days when he was already a follower of Jesus. As a matter of fact, John baptized his unpleasantness in righteous concepts: He wanted to destroy a city because he felt they had slighted Jesus, and he rebuked those who were casting out demons because he wanted to keep the Kingdom pure. John grew into the love that made him beautiful. His salvation came in a grand moment of decision, but his transformation— at least, as far as outward evidences are concerned—came in a long period of living with the love of God in Jesus Christ.

There's a bit of thunder in all of us; more in some, less in others. There is in all of us a readiness to burn up people and to push others aside while seeking our own advancement. So we look with awe at the apostle John, a son of thunder who became the apostolic synonym for love. And we pray—"Don't give up on me, Dear Lord. See a potential in me that others (and I, myself) may not have noticed. And bring it to fruition. Please, bring it to fruition! Amen."

CHAPTER 13

$\mathcal{M}$ATTHIAS, HOLY SUBSTITUTE

READ ACTS 1:15-26.

Maybe I'm guilty of some irrational prejudice in including Matthias in this book. I confess that I know of no other book on the apostles that gives him a chapter. A faithful researcher tells me, after examining scores of books on the disciples, that most don't even mention Matthias's name—and those who do, give him only the briefest reference.

Yet I've always been somewhat taken by Matthias. Maybe it's a kind of scholarly tidiness, one that insists on treating him simply because the book of Acts names him as the successor to Judas Iscariot. Or perhaps I'm taken by his underdog role. Perhaps there is a tie with some dark corner of my psyche. I remember rather frequent occasions early in my ministry when someone would telephone, "We're having this meeting in two weeks. We've tried everywhere to get a speaker, and they've all turned us down. Then we thought of you. Would you be able to come?" Maybe that gave me a Matthias complex, the feeling of being a blessed afterthought.

No matter! I find Matthias interesting, perhaps even compelling, so I'm asking you to look at him with me.

He has only one brief entry in Scripture, in the book of Acts, but it's clear from that reference that he was part of the larger apostolic band from the very beginning. After the resurrection of our Lord, the disciples were preoccupied simply in their meetings with him, but following Jesus' ascension into heaven, they settled in to do business. Mind you, it was truly holy business; the writer of Acts tells us that they "were constantly devoting themselves to prayer" (Acts 1:14). Then they faced their first real administrative decision. How should they replace Judas Iscariot?

You and I might wonder why they even saw such a need. After all, the company of the apostles was not like an athletic team where there must always be a certain number of players on the field. Nor is there any indication that their body was so structured that each person had an assignment that only that person could fulfill. True, if they were going to go out two-by-two, as the seventy had done (see Luke 10:1-16), eleven would be an uneven number, but that idea is nowhere suggested.

From the disciples' point of view, the issues were much more far-reaching. As Simon Peter outlined the matter to the body, he quoted from the Hebrew Scriptures; first, to set Judas's act in a context (see Acts 1:20 and Psalm 69:25). Then, to authorize their next step, Peter directed their attention to Psalm 109:8—"Let another take his position of overseer" (see Acts 1:20). Often the New Testament writers quoted passages from the Old Testament because they saw unfolding events as fulfillment of ancient promises and prophecies. It's hard to know if Simon Peter had such a purpose in mind in this instance, or whether he was simply saying, "We have a vacancy to be filled." But even if only the latter, he wanted the group to know that the actions they were about to take possessed holy significance.

Still more important, I'm sure, was the divine importance that was often given to numbers. Twelve was not simply a number to a faithful Jew; it was the number of Jacob's sons, and therefore the number of the twelve tribes of Israel. And even though ten of those tribes had long been dispersed and lost through intermarriage, the Jews still saw themselves as a people of twelve tribes. A scattering of persons from the ten northern tribes had emigrated over time to the south, so that even if a statistical case was weak, it was still possible to argue mystically that the twelve tribes were even yet constituted in the remaining tribes that made up the southern kingdom of Judah, or the Jews.

No doubt the disciples saw significance in their number. They were "the twelve"; the four Gospels refer to them by that name roughly twenty times. Jesus added specific significance to their number when he told them, at a particularly crucial time, "Truly I tell you, at the renewal of all things, when the Son of Man is seated on the throne of his glory, you who have followed me will also sit on twelve thrones, judging the twelve tribes of Israel" (Matthew 19:28).

One never knows how well the disciples caught the importance of Jesus' words; it's clear enough, in many instances, that they were dull of hearing. But statements of the sort I've just quoted must surely have caught their attention. They must have looked around their rather motley collection of fishermen, tax collector, and latent revolutionaries and muttered to themselves, " 'Judging the twelve tribes?' this has to be the beginning of something *big!*" Big, indeed, the beginning of a new Israel.

So the absence of one of their number, by the defection of Judas, wasn't simply a reduction of 8.3 percent, it was a violation of a holy symmetry. Therefore it must be remedied, and without delay. *We* might say, "So, once there were twelve, and now it's eleven; let's just close ranks, and make the most of it." But not these men steeped in Jewish faith and tradition. For them, twelve was a number of divine identity, a number that had been given crucial new importance by Jesus in their choosing. One can imagine the discussion becoming more animated as one of them recalled, "And when the Master fed the five thousand, it was twelve baskets that we picked up afterward" (see Matthew 14:20), and another saying, "And on the night of Jesus' betrayal, he said that if he wanted, he could call for twelve legions of angels" (see Matthew 26:53). Yes, there must be twelve; not eleven or thirteen, but *twelve!* It is interesting to see the way the number has continued its influence in our Western culture. We buy things, and count them, by the *dozen*, by twelve. Ten would be a better number, since it fits our decimal system, but we are inheritors of the biblical story, even when we go to the bakery or pick up a carton of eggs.

So while it may seem to us that the disciples were a bit hurried in their pursuit of a successor to Judas, for the eleven, it was the first order of business. Modern peace negotiations begin with the size and shape of the table and the seating order of the participants, a process that of itself sometimes seems interminable; for the disciples, the first concern was to restore their number to its primary and ultimate significance.

In our day, many Bible students feel the disciples erred. One suggests that this was an example of Peter's impetuosity; he acted first and thought later. Many feel that the true replacement for Judas proved to be Saul of Tarsus—later rechristened as Paul, the apostle—and that the disciples should have waited until the Holy Spirit made the divine will known simply by raising up the proper person.

But I go with the apostles. I'm absolutely sure they acted in good faith. It's also clear that they proceeded only after much prayer. Now mind you, I've lived long enough to know that persons can act in good faith, even after having prayed, and still do willful and unwise things. Sincerity is no excuse, though heaven knows most of us have used it from time to time.

As for the argument that the records give no evidence that Matthias ever amounted to anything, I will be equally pragmatic and make the same comment about Thaddaeus, or James the Less. For that matter, as we have already seen, none of the original twelve gets any really substantial hearing in the book of Acts except Peter and John, and even John slips quietly from that particular scene.

I'll admit, too, that I have a prejudice against Monday-morning quarterbacks. It's always easy to say that the ball should have been fed off to the tight end when you're sitting at the television screen, watching the fifth replay, and not worried about a long ton of humanity aiming to destroy you. It's one thing to speculate twenty centuries later about what the disciples should have done, but such speculation is utterly irrelevant. They were closer to the scene, obviously, than we are now, and they had a better view of the real playing field than we do. What they did made sense at the time the decision had to be made.

And as a matter of fact, they proceeded in quite sensible fashion. They established an impeccable standard. They looked for someone who had "accompanied us during all the time that the Lord Jesus went in and out among us, beginning from the baptism of John until the day when he was taken up from us" (Acts 1:21-22). By this standard, incidentally, the apostle Paul could not have qualified—a fact that he himself noted when he described himself as one "untimely born" (1 Corinthians 15:8).

Apparently Matthias was a true seeker. He must have been one of those persons whose quest for truth led him to John the Baptist, and from there to Christ. There came a time when numbers of persons who had once affiliated with Jesus "turned back," so that Jesus asked, "Do you also wish to go away?" (John 6:66-67). Matthias was one of those who stayed. We can assume that he was somewhere in the crowds at the Crucifixion, and that he also saw the resurrected Christ, because of course resurrection was the key message. The one who was to be chosen, Peter said, "must become a witness with us to his [Jesus'] resurrection" (Acts 1:22). And, as already noted in the words of Peter, Matthias had been present at the time of Jesus' ascension.

So Matthias was no chance option. He wasn't a rookie lately arrived at training camp. Tradition says that Matthias was one of the seventy that Jesus sent out "ahead of him in pairs to every town and place where he himself intended to go" (Luke 10:1). It surely seems likely. And if that be the case, Matthias received some valuable and exciting experience prior to the events in the book of Acts.

What bothers many more modern readers, of course, is the method by which Matthias was selected from among the two finalists. The disciples found two persons who fulfilled all of the requirements, and who seemed to them to be qualified, Matthias and Joseph Barsabbas. Then they prayed briefly and pointedly for God's guidance and cast lots—"and the lot fell on Matthias" (Acts 1:26). One biblical student writes this method of selection off as "superstition." But superstition, like beauty, is in the eye of the beholder.

The disciples were following in the best of their tradition. In the Old Testament, the lot—some object—was used for everything from the distribution of land among the twelve tribes to selecting the roles of the ritual goats on the Day of Atonement. Casting lots was to be an act done reverently, before God, in pursuit of God's guidance. Thus the writer of Proverbs says, "The lot is cast into the lap, / but the decision is the LORD's alone" (16:33).

I'm not recommending the use of the lot (although when I think of some of the politicking I've seen during the election of some officials, the lot looks rather attractive). But neither will I pass judgment on the way the disciples used it in the selection of Matthias, or on the result of their use. The most incisive comment about the lot is that it is never referred to after the Day of Pentecost, from which some draw the conclusion that thereafter the church was supposed to use the more direct guidance of the Holy Spirit. Again, I demur slightly when I reflect on how badly I've seen the Holy Spirit quoted over the years, and when I consider the quite casual way people say "the Lord led me" or "the Lord told me." No, I'm not recommending the lot. I'm only saying that I think the apostles were right in what they did; and also, that you and I should be very cautious in *any* instances where we seek to declare the will of God.

So Matthias "was added to the eleven apostles," and that's the last the New Testament tells us about him. Nor has he found a large place in the traditions of the church. Broadly speaking, there are two traditions. One says that he conducted his entire ministry in Jerusalem and was finally buried there. The other, more prevalent, tradition says that he ministered in Africa, first with the Ethiopians, then in Arabia Felix and on the coasts of the Red Sea. One story has him working with a cannibal tribe in Africa, nearly losing his life there. The Greeks believed that he preached in Colchis, an ancient country south of the Caucasus and bordering on the Black Sea. He is said to be the only apostle whose remains are in Germany, although his skull is preserved in Italy. I choose to let his remains lie in peace, wherever.

But several matters impress me. I wonder, for one, how it felt to succeed Judas. Did this association cast shadows of a type across Matthias's life? I knew a good man once whose bishop sent him to a church where the two previous pastors had been guilty of moral infractions. He said that when he arrived, some people asked, with a bit of pathos, what might happen to him. Speaking of superstition, as we did a while ago, I venture Matthias had to deal with it in some very personal ways.

I think I especially like Matthias because he followed Jesus all of his life without attention or accolades, except, it appears, for the brief hour when he was named to the Twelve. When Jesus named the original twelve, Matthias saw persons selected whose credentials perhaps were no better than his; after all, he too had been present from the beginning. I wonder if he suffered any painful moments when Simon Peter, Andrew, James—his old friends—became part of the select company, while he was left on the fringe. Perhaps it was the fringe of the seventy, but it's far more exciting to be part of the twelve or the three than to be one of seventy! If any of this bothered Matthias, it didn't find much expression, else he wouldn't have passed the selection process that narrowed down to him and Joseph Barsabbas.

However tenuous was Matthias's claim, he was named an apostle. He was a holy substitute, and if he hit no game-winning home runs, he nevertheless played his post. Most of us know what it is, at one time or another, to be a second choice—for the prom, for a team, for a promotion, a friendship, or even a spouse.

The issue ultimately is not *when* we are chosen, but *that* we are chosen—and beyond that, what we do with our role after it comes to us. If we come to our place late, far down the line (it appears) of choices, let us do our task so well that persons will always wonder why we weren't chosen first. Such is the unique honor of a holy substitute.

Study Guide

Suggestions for Leading a Study of *The Thirteen Apostles*

John D. Schroeder

This book is designed to help readers get to know the thirteen apostles better. To assist you in facilitating a discussion group, this study guide was created to help make this experience beneficial for both you and the members of your group. Here are some thoughts on how you can help your group:

1. Distribute the book to participants before your first meeting and request that they come having read the introduction and chapter 1. You may want to limit the size of your group to increase participation.

2. Begin your sessions on time. Your participants will appreciate your promptness. You may want to begin your first session with introductions and a brief get-acquainted time. Start each session by reading aloud the snapshot summary of the chapter for the day.

3. Select discussion questions and activities in advance. Note that the first question is a general question designed to get discussion going. Feel free to change the order of the listed questions and to create your own questions. Allow a set amount of time for the questions and activities.

4. Remind your participants that all questions are valid as part of the learning process. Encourage their participation in discussion by saying that there are no "wrong" answers and that all input will be appreciated. Invite them to share their thoughts, personal stories, and ideas as their comfort level allows.

5. Some questions may be more difficult to answer than others. If you ask a question and no one responds, begin the discussion by venturing an answer yourself. Then ask for comments and other answers. Remember that some questions may have multiple answers.

6. Ask the questions "Why?" or "Why do you believe that?" to help continue a discussion and give it greater depth.

7. Give everyone a chance to talk. Keep the conversation moving. Occasionally you may want to direct a question to a specific person who has been quiet. "Do you have anything to add?" is a good follow-up question to ask another person. If the topic of conversation gets off track, move ahead by asking the next question in your study guide.

8. Before moving from questions to activities, ask group members if they have any questions that have not been answered. Remember that as a leader, you do not have to know all the answers. Some answers may come from group members. Other answers may even need a bit of research. Your job is to keep the discussion moving and to encourage participation.

9. Review the activity in advance. Feel free to modify it or to create your own activity. Encourage participants to try the "At home" activity.

10. Following the conclusion of the activity, close with a brief prayer, praying either the printed prayer from the study guide or a prayer of your own. If your group desires, pause for individual prayer petitions.

11. Be grateful and supportive. Thank group members for their ideas and participation.
12. You are not expected to be a "perfect" leader. Just do the best you can by focusing on the participants and the lesson. God will help you lead this group.
13. Enjoy your time together.

Suggestions for Participants

1. What you will receive from this study will be in direct proportion to your involvement. Be an active participant!
2. Please make a point to attend all sessions and to arrive on time so that you can receive the greatest benefit.
3. Read the chapter and review the study-guide questions prior to the meeting. You may want to jot down questions you have from the reading and also answers to some of the study-guide questions.
4. Be supportive and appreciative of your group leader as well as other members of your group. You are on a journey together.
5. Your participation is encouraged. Feel free to share your thoughts about the material being discussed.
6. Pray for your group and your leader.

Chapter 1

ANDREW, A BROTHER

Snapshot Summary

This chapter tells us about Andrew, his role as a brother, and the impact he made as an apostle.

Discussion Questions

1. What insights did you receive from this chapter?
2. Why do you think Andrew was the first person to be called by Jesus to be an apostle?
3. Why is the word *brother* tied to Andrew's identity?
4. According to the author, "we use the word *brother* primarily in two ways"; what are those two meanings of the word, and how do they apply to Andrew?
5. What do we know about Andrew's background before he became an apostle?
6. "Andrew was a person of spiritual hunger"; explain what the author means by this. *always seeking* •
7. What does it mean to possess the spirit of a brother?
8. Who did Andrew first tell after he found Jesus? Why do you think he did this?
9. What are the three stories of Andrew found in the Gospel of John?
10. According to tradition, where did Andrew preach? How did he die?

Activities

As a group: Discuss the qualities and behavioral traits of Andrew that we should possess as Christians.

At *home*: Practice being a "brother" to others during the com‐ing week.

Prayer: *Dear God, thank you for this study of your apostle Andrew. Help us to be Christian brothers to others as Andrew was. May we have the same spiritual hunger as Andrew, and may we find our satisfaction in you. Amen.*

Chapter 2

PETER, MAN OF ACTION

Snapshot Summary

This chapter explores the life of Simon Peter, a man of action who wasn't always right, but loved his Lord and worked to carry on Jesus' ministry.

Discussion Questions

1. What insights did you receive from this chapter?
2. What is known of Simon's Peter's background before he became an apostle?
3. Describe the character and personality of Peter.
4. Give an example of how Peter was a man of action.
5. What were some of Peter's notable mistakes?
6. What was probably the highest moment in Peter's life? Explain.
7. Discuss Peter's words and deeds during the events sur‐rounding the Crucifixion.
8. How was Peter a leader and a spokesman after the Crucifixion?
9. How do we sometimes act and sound like Peter today?
10. What does tradition tell us about Peter's death?

Activities

As a group: Discuss how we can be people of action in the modern church. What are the costs and benefits of being people of action?

At home: Meditate on the life of Peter. Reflect on your own actions as a Christian.

Prayer: *Dear God, thank you for this study of your apostle Peter. Help us to take action on your behalf in our world today, knowing that you love and support us. Amen.*

Chapter 3

JAMES, UNFULFILLED LEADER

Snapshot Summary

This chapter examines the life of James, a disciple with great leadership potential and ambition, whose early death cut short his ministry.

Discussion Questions

1. What insights did you receive from this chapter?
2. What do we know about James's early life and his background?
3. Describe the personality and behavioral traits of James.
4. What do you think motivated James to follow Jesus?
5. Why were James and John called "Sons of Thunder" by Jesus?
6. How did James react to a problem with the Samaritans in Luke 9:54?

7. Why do you think James was a member of Jesus' inner circle?
8. Discuss the strengths and weaknesses of James as a leader.
9. What role did ambition play in James's ministry? Did it hurt or help? What role should ambition play in the life of a Christian?
10. How was James a leader at the hour of his death?

Activities

As a group: Discuss the theory that there is a bit of James in most of us; give some examples relating to words and deeds of Christians today.
At home: Reflect on how James's pilgrimage to God is like your own. Think about what you can learn from the life of this apostle.

Prayer: *Dear God, thank you for this study of your apostle James. Help us to be leaders at home, work, church, and in our community. May we share your love with others and be your disciples as we minister to those in need. Amen.*

Chapter 4

PHILIP, THE DELIBERATE

Snapshot Summary

This chapter explores the life of Philip, an apostle whose words and deeds were deliberate, who thrived on information and research, yet was a loving and dedicated follower of Jesus.

Discussion Questions

1. What insights did you receive from this chapter?
2. What was unusual about the name of Philip?
3. Share what you know of Philip's background and early life.
4. Give some details about the personality of Philip.
5. What qualities do you think led Jesus to choose Philip as one of the twelve apostles?
6. Recall Philip's part in the story of the feeding of the five thousand. What do you think was the significance of that role?
7. What do we know about Philip's integrity as revealed when the Greeks approached him?
8. It has been said that Philip had "a warm heart and a pessimistic head"; what does this mean?
9. How has the name *Philip* left a mark in our culture?
10. What is the only thing we know, with some certainty, about Philip's later ministry and death?

Activities

As a group: How did being a deliberate person both help and hurt Philip's ministry?
At home: Reflect on how you can be either more or less deliberate in your own life. Are you too pessimistic or not pessimistic enough?

Prayer: *Dear God, thank you for this study of your apostle Philip. Help us to remember that you have need and work for every temperament and every personality. We all belong to you, and you love us just as we are. Amen.*

Chapter 5

JAMES THE LESS

Snapshot Summary

This chapter explores the life of James, an apostle who was faithful, but often forgotten and overlooked.

Discussion Questions

1. What insights did you receive from this chapter?
2. How many times is James mentioned in the Bible, and under what circumstances?
3. As the author points out, what type of home did James probably come from?
4. What are the two names for James? Why were these used by Jesus and by the other apostles?
5. What is it like to be unnoticed? Recall a time when you felt overlooked.
6. In what ways was James a fortunate human being?
7. Since Jesus called James to be an apostle, what does that say about James? What does it say about Jesus?
8. What can be assumed about the ministry of James?
9. What can we learn from James concerning accomplishment?
10. What does legend say about James's death?

Activities

As a group: Discuss why the Bible does not say more about James or his ministry. What other people in the Bible are similar to James in that we know little about them?

At home: Reflect this week on people who live their lives unnoticed. What value do they bring to others? Why are they unnoticed? What people in your church are unnoticed?

Prayer: *Dear God, thank you for this study of your apostle James "the Less," an unnoticed but faithful follower. Help us to remember that all believers are special in your sight, and that you love us all and appreciate our uniqueness. Amen.*

Chapter 6

SIMON, THE ZEALOT

Snapshot Summary

This chapter examines the life of Simon the Zealot, a political activist who was attracted to Jesus' leadership with mixed motives, but stayed with Jesus because Jesus became his ultimate loyalty.

Discussion Questions

1. What new insights did you receive from this chapter?
2. Explain what a Zealot was and what they believed.
3. What things do you think motivated Simon?
4. How did the last of the Zealots die?
5. Why do you think Simon was drawn to Jesus?
6. What kind of adjustments did Simon have to make in order to coexist with the other apostles, especially Matthew?
7. How is the Christian church today like the band of twelve apostles?
8. What lessons can we learn from Simon?
9. Noting the ways in which Simon was influenced by others, what people and events have influenced and changed your life?
10. What does tradition tell us about Simon and his ministry after the Resurrection?

Activities

As a group: Discuss the topic of motives. What motivates us to join a certain church or to be passionate about a cause within the church? What motivates us as Christians?

At home: Reflect this week on how God meets us where we are and speaks to us in the circumstances of our unique and individual lives.

Prayer: *Dear God, thank you for this study of your apostle Simon. Help us to realize the ways in which we are like Simon. We all follow you with different expectations and motives. Our understanding may be limited, but help us nevertheless to love you in fullness, as Simon did. In Jesus' name, Amen.*

Chapter 7

NATHANAEL, THE FORTHRIGHT

Snapshot Summary

This chapter looks at the life of Nathanael, the apostle with the childlike quality of directness.

Discussion Questions

1. What insights did you receive from this chapter?
2. What do we know about Nathanael before he became an apostle?
3. Why do we refer to this apostle as both Nathanael and Bartholomew?
4. Share a time when you were forthright. What was the result?
5. How did Philip introduce Nathanael to Jesus?

6. Why did Nathanael say, "Can anything good come out of Nazareth?" and how did Philip respond?
7. What did Jesus say to Nathanael? What did Jesus see in him?
8. What did Jesus imply when he said that he had seen Nathanael under the fig tree?
9. What can we learn from Nathanael?
10. What do legend and tradition say about Nathanael after the Crucifixion?

Activities

As a group: Discuss the pros and cons of being forthright. What causes us not to be direct with others as adults? Do you want others to be direct with you? Why or why not?
At home: Try to be forthright with people this week. Report the results to your study group next week.

Prayer: *Dear God, thank you for this study of your apostle Nathanael. May we learn from his ministry and his personality. Help us to have openness and enthusiasm in our ministry to others. Amen.*

Chapter 8

MATTHEW, THE SUCCESSFUL MAN

Snapshot Summary

This chapter explores success and what it means through the life of the apostle Matthew.

Discussion Questions

1. What insights did you receive from this chapter?
2. How do *you* define a successful person?
3. How were tax collectors regarded in Matthew's day?
4. How did Jesus see Matthew? What did he see that others did not see?
5. Why was Matthew an unlikely choice for an apostle?
6. Why, does the author suggest, was Matthew able to hear the voice of God? What often drowns out the voice of God?
7. Why do you think Matthew accepted Jesus' call to be an apostle?
8. What can we learn from the life of Matthew?
9. How is Matthew thought of today? How will he be regarded years from now?
10. What does tradition say happened to Matthew after the Resurrection?

Activities

As a group: Discuss the pros and cons of having money and being successful. How do you think great wealth affects a person's life?

At home: Reflect on your relationship with God. Has success had an impact on you? What are you seeking that you have not yet achieved?

Prayer: *Dear God, thank you for study of your apostle Matthew, and for showing us what we can learn from his words and deeds. Help us to remember both what is important and what is not important in this life. Amen.*

Chapter 9

THOMAS, TWENTY-FIRST-CENTURY MAN

Snapshot Summary

This chapter examines the life of Thomas, an apostle who searched for facts and found Jesus.

Discussion Questions

1. What insights did you receive from this chapter?
2. According to the author, how are human beings the same in every century?
3. How was Thomas different from the other apostles? How was he similar to them?
4. How did first-century people deal with life's mysteries? How do we deal with life's mysteries today?
5. Why does the author say Thomas was a twenty-first-century man? Do you agree with this characterization of a twenty-first-century human being?
6. What do we know about Thomas's name and his background?
7. Reflect on / discuss the story of Thomas and Lazarus.
8. Reflect on / discuss the story of Thomas at the Last Supper.
9. Reflect on / discuss the story of "Doubting Thomas" after the Resurrection.
10. According to tradition, what did Thomas do after the Resurrection? Where did he preach? How did he die?

Activities

As a group: Discuss how we are all like "Doubting Thomas." What does God want us to do with our doubts?

At *home:* Reflect on the life of Thomas. Consider how you handle doubts and your need for evidence and facts.

Prayer: *Dear God, thank you for this study of your apostle Thomas. Help us to learn from his life and his actions. May we replace doubt with belief, as we replace fear with the knowledge of your love and presence. In Jesus' name. Amen.*

Chapter 10

THADDAEUS, THE QUESTIONER

Snapshot Summary

This chapter looks at the life of Thaddaeus, an inconspicuous apostle, known for asking Jesus a question.

Discussion Questions

1. What insights did you receive from this chapter?
2. What other names was Thaddaeus known by? Why was he known by more than one name? Which may have been his true name?
3. What legend of the birth of Jesus involves Thaddaeus?
4. Describe the distinction the author makes between the meaning of the words *average* and *mediocre*. Why, does he suggest, is "average" not necessarily so bad?
5. Do you consider yourself "average," or "ordinary"? Why or why not?
6. How is the modern church like the twelve apostles?
7. According to the author, what is the value of asking questions and the value of people who ask questions?
8. What question did Thaddaeus ask Jesus, and why? How did Jesus reply?

9. Why is Thaddaeus known as Saint Jude?
10. What is known about the ministry of Thaddaeus after the Resurrection?

Activities

As a group: Discuss this statement: Jesus worked with ordinary people. Do you agree? Do ordinary Christians have an impact on others? Are we all basically the same? How are some Christians different from others?
At home: Reflect on the message of Jesus' reply to Thaddaeus: *When someone loves me, he or she will follow my teachings* (see John 14:23-24).

Prayer: *Dear God, thank you for this study of your apostle Thaddaeus. Help us to continue to ask the right questions as we strive to grow in faith. Amen.*

Chapter 11

JUDAS, THE VALUE OF A DOLLAR

Snapshot Summary

This chapter looks at the life of Judas Iscariot, the apostle who betrayed Jesus.

Discussion Questions

1. What insights did you receive from this chapter?
2. What is known about the background of Judas?
3. What position did Judas have in the group? What were his duties?

4. What does the name Judas mean? What does his name tell us?
5. What factors may have caused Judas to betray Jesus?
6. Do you feel some sympathy for Judas? Why or why not?
7. Why do you think Judas kissed Jesus with such intensity when he betrayed him?
8. What was Judas's strength? Judas's weakness?
9. What did Judas do after betraying Jesus? What should he have done instead? Why didn't he?
10. What does Judas remind us about ourselves?

Activities

As a group: Discuss whether or not Judas was essential to the divine plan. Was he a divine catalyst? Was he helpless to resist evil?
At home: Reflect on your own strengths and weaknesses.

Prayer: *Dear God, thank you for the lessons we learn from your apostles. Thank you for giving us the opportunity and the insight to reflect on our own behavior as Christians, both our faults and our strengths. Help us to remember your love, and that you are with us always. Amen.*

Chapter 12

JOHN, LOVE AND THUNDER

Snapshot Summary

This chapter examines the dynamic character and personality of the apostle John, and it shows us how the love of Jesus can change us over the years.

Discussion Questions

1. What insights did you receive from this chapter?
2. What do we know about John before he became an apostle?
3. How did John change over the years? What caused him to change?
4. Describe the nature of John's "thunder" remarks (Luke 9:51-56; Mark 10:35-45; Mark 9:38).
5. Give some examples of remarks attributed to John regarding love?
6. Why was it so important to John for us to love one another?
7. How did John react to someone casting out demons in Jesus' name? How do we react in similar ways today? Why is this so?
8. What did Jesus mean in Mark 9:39-40 in replying to John's concern?
9. According to tradition, what happened to John on the Isle of Patmos?
10. What else does tradition tell us about John?

Activities

As a group: We are told to love one another. It sounds so simple, so why is it so difficult? Discuss the importance of loving others. Share what both Jesus and John say in the Bible about loving one another.

At home: Reflect on how you have changed over the years, and consider the reasons for it. Reflect on how you want to continue to grow.

Prayer: *Dear God, thank you for this study of your apostle John. Help us to grow in love toward you and toward one another. Replace our thunder with words and actions of love. Amen.*

Chapter 13

MATTHIAS, HOLY SUBSTITUTE

Snapshot Summary

This final chapter tells us about Matthias, the successor to Judas Iscariot.

Discussion Questions

1. What insights did you receive from this chapter?
2. For what reasons does the author include Matthias in this book?
3. How is Matthias mentioned in the Bible?
4. Why was the number twelve significant to the disciples?
5. For what reasons did the disciples feel the need to replace Judas?
6. Who do some feel the true replacement for Judas eventually proved to be, and why?
7. What do we know about Matthias and his qualifications?
8. Who were the two finalists for the vacant position among the apostles? How was the final selection made, and why was this method chosen?
9. Do you think it would have bothered Matthias that he had not been chosen as one of the original twelve apostles? Why or why not?
10. What does tradition say about the ministry of Matthias?

Activities

As a group: Share what you have learned from this book and from one another during your study of the thirteen apostles. How have your views changed, or how have they been reinforced? How do you now view the apostles? What particular

topic or which apostle(s) made the biggest impact on you?
At home: Reflect on the thirteen apostles—their successes, their faults, their faith and ministry. Reflect on your own calling as a Christian disciple of Jesus Christ.

Prayer: *Dear God, thank you for this study of the apostles. Thank you for the insights you have provided us into the lives of the apostles, and for the insights you have given us into our own lives as well. Strengthen us all in love toward you and toward one another. In Jesus' name. Amen.*

17203842R00073

Made in the USA
Lexington, KY
29 August 2012